Everybody ...

'Is it possible to run a successful business without treating people like numbers? Can a corporate culture of mistrust and insecurity be transformed into one of caring and fulfilment? *Everybody Matters* answers these questions with an enthusiastic "Yes!" If you're ready for a new way of doing business, this is the book for you'
Daniel H. Pink, author, *To Sell is Human* and *Drive*

'It is almost impossible for me to adequately convey my admiration, excitement and incredulity . . . To give people the power and freedom to care for each other, to trust that people want to do well and be good . . . and to see how these things create value for everyone – it doesn't get better than that. I have (happy) tears in my eyes as I write this'
Amy Cuddy, associate professor, Harvard Business School

'*Everybody Matters* simply blew me away. This is THE book that practically every corporate CEO in North America has been breathlessly waiting for . . . even if they don't yet know it!'
Bob Burg, co-author, *The Go-Giver*

'When it comes to maximizing potential, Chapman and his team at Barry-Wehmiller have it figured it out. This deeply moving and practical book will have you asking yourself "Why haven't we been doing this?" Now you can begin tomorrow!'
Jack Canfield, co-author, *Chicken Soup for the Soul*®
At Work and *The Success Principles*™

'Profit matters, but people matter more. Bob Chapman and Raj Sisodia use real-world examples to illustrate how the humanity so often absent in today's boardrooms is actually a direct path to sustained growth. It's a message that should be taken to heart by business leaders everywhere'
Ron Shaich, founder, chairman and CEO, Panera Bread

'Bob and Raj beautifully illustrate the important intersection of business and the true essence of the human spirit. One company, one employee at a time, Barry-Wehmiller is changing the world – and the world of business! If this model can be successful in many . . . everywhere'
Ki . . . Store

ABOUT THE AUTHORS

Bob Chapman is the Chairman and CEO of Barry-Wehmiller, a global capital equipment and engineering consulting company. A combination of almost eighty acquired companies spread among ten operating divisions around the world, Barry-Wehmiller's vision is to use the power of business to build a better world. Chapman blogs about leadership and culture at www.trulyhumanleadership.com.

Raj Sisodia is the FW Olin Distinguished Professor of Global Business and Whole Foods Market Research Scholar in Conscious Capitalism at Babson College. His most recent book is the *Wall Street Journal* bestseller *Conscious Capitalism* (with John P. Mackey, co-founder and co-CEO of Whole Foods Market).

For more information visit www.Barry-Wehmiller.com or www.BWLeadershipInstitute.com

Everybody
Matters

The Extraordinary Power of Caring for
Your People Like Family

BOB CHAPMAN
AND RAJ SISODIA

PORTFOLIO
PENGUIN

PORTFOLIO PENGUIN

UK | USA | Canada | Ireland | Australia
India | New Zealand | South Africa

Portfolio Penguin is part of the Penguin Random House group of companies
whose addresses can be found at global.penguinrandomhouse.com.

First published in the United States of America by Portfolio/Penguin,
a member of Penguin Group (USA) Inc. 2015
First published in Great Britain by Portfolio Penguin 2015
001

Printed in Great Britain by Clays Ltd, St Ives plc

A CIP catalogue record for this book is available from the British Library

ISBN: 978-0-241-97540-4

www.greenpenguin.co.uk

Penguin Random House is committed to a
sustainable future for our business, our readers
and our planet. This book is made from Forest
Stewardship Council® certified paper.

To my parents, Bill and Marjorie Chapman, for their unconditional love and trust during my journey; to Rev. Edward Salmon Jr. for awaking in me a higher purpose; and to my wife, Cynthia, for her unconditional love and support of our dedication to bringing about a more caring world.

—BOB CHAPMAN

To the extraordinary architects of cultural transformation at Barry-Wehmiller: Rhonda Spencer, Brian Wellinghoff, Sara Hannah, and David VanderMolen. Your dedication to uplifting all the lives Barry-Wehmiller touches is truly inspiring. Without you, this book would not exist.

—RAJ SISODIA

Contents

Foreword

"Our people matter," says nearly every CEO on the face of the planet. "Without our people," so the logic goes, "we would not achieve our goals."

Rare are the leaders of organizations who will tell you that their people don't matter. However, there is a big difference between understanding the value of the people inside an organization and actually making decisions that consider their needs. It's like saying, "my kids are my priority," but always putting work first. What kind of family dynamic or relationship with our kids do we think results?

The same is true in business. When we say our people matter but we don't actually care for them, it can shatter trust and create a culture of paranoia, cynicism, and self-interest. This is not some highfalutin management theory—it's biology. We are social animals and we respond to the environments we're in. Good people put in a bad environment are capable of doing bad things. People who may have done bad things, put in a good environment, are capable of becoming remarkable, trustworthy, and valuable members of an organization. This is why leadership matters. Leaders set the culture. Leaders are responsible for overseeing the environment in which people are asked to work . . . and the people will act in accordance with that culture.

Culture equals values plus behavior, as my friend Lt. Gen. George Flynn, USMC (ret.) says. If an organization has a strong and clearly stated set of values and the people act in accordance with those values, then the culture will be strong. If, however, the values are ill-defined, constantly changing, or the people aren't held accountable to or incentivized to uphold those values, then the culture will be weak. It's no good putting "honesty" or "integrity" on the wall if we aren't willing to confront people who consistently fail to uphold those values, regardless of their performance. Failure to do so sends a message to everyone else in the organization—"it doesn't matter if you're dishonest or act with questionable integrity, as long as you make your numbers." The result is a culture of people who will drive for short-term results while systematically dismantling any sense of trust and cooperation. It's just the way people react to the environment they are in. And without trust and cooperation, innovation suffers, productivity lags, and consistent, long-term success never really materializes. The worst-case scenarios often end in crimes being committed, sleight-of-hand accounting practices, or serious ethics violations. But the more familiar scenarios include office politics, gossip, paranoia, and stress.

I admit I am an idealist. I understand that it is a lot easier for me to say and write things like "put your people first" than it is to actually put it into practice. Financial pressures, pressure from the competition, pressure from the board, the media, Wall Street, internal politics, ego . . . the list goes on . . . all factor into why sometimes well-meaning leaders of organizations don't (or can't, as some say) care about their people like human beings instead of managing them like assets.

That's why Bob Chapman matters.

If you ask Bob what his company does, he will tell you, "We build great people who do extraordinary things." If you ask him how he measures his results, he will tell you, "We measure success by the way we touch the lives of people." It all sounds rather fluffy and mushy. But for the fact that he means it—and it works. Because if you ask Bob what fuels his company, only then will he talk about the financials. And on that level, the amount of fuel Chapman's companies are able to produce would be the envy of most CEOs.

When I first met Bob, he told me he was building a company that looked like what I talk about. Again, I'm an idealist. I believe it's important to strive for the things I speak and write about . . . achieving it is an entirely different thing. And so I told Bob, the very first time we met, "I want to see it." And see it I did!

We crossed the country visiting various offices and factories and in all cases Bob let me wander around and talk to whomever I wanted. I was free to ask any questions. He stayed out of all the meetings and he wasn't with us when we took the factory tours. And what I saw was nothing short of astounding. I saw people come to tears when talking about how much they loved their jobs. I heard stories of people who used to hate going to work, who didn't trust management, who now love going to work and see management as their partners.

I saw safe, clean factories, not because of some management-imposed safety or cleanliness program. The factories were safe and the machines well looked after because the people who worked there cared about their equipment and each other. I could go on and on . . . but it's probably better if you read the book.

I've since taken others to see Barry-Wehmiller's offices and factories, and the results are always the same. People are blown away by what Chapman has created. As for me? I can no longer be accused of being an idealist if what I imagine exists in reality.

It begs the question, if what I talk and write about can exist in reality, if every C-level executive acknowledges the importance and value of people, why is Bob Chapman and Barry-Wehmiller the exception rather than the rule? The reason, once again, is pressure. Though nearly every CEO on the planet talks about the importance of doing things for the long term and the value of long-term results, an uncomfortably high number don't seem to run their companies that way. Forget about ten- or twenty-year plans, the quarter or the year is king. Even if a five-year plan exits, odds are it gets changed or abandoned within those five years. It's hard to make a strong argument to defend the way so many leaders of organizations conduct business today.

Though a lot of leaders talk about this stuff, in *Everybody Matters* you will see what happens when you actually do it. You will learn what happens when leaders care about the lives of the people inside the company as if they were family, Truly Human Leadership, as Bob Chapman calls it. You will also learn about the remarkable power unleashed when leadership is aligned with a long-term vision. That single ability is what allows for the patience to do the right thing. That combined with a desire to do right by the people is what makes companies great. And I think we need a few more great companies in the world today.

Simon Sinek

Optimist

Author of *Start With Why* and *Leaders Eat Last*

Prologue

|A Passion for People|

"It was definitely a low point in my life," recalled Ken Coppens. As a laid-off production worker for Paper Converting Machine Company (PCMC) in Green Bay, Wisconsin, with a wife and young son, Ken was resorting to whatever legal means he could find to make ends meet. It was game day at Lambeau Field. Midway into the third quarter, Ken, dressed in layers, grabbed two black heavy-duty trash bags and began the three-block walk from his house to the stadium. With any luck, Packers fans would have left behind enough recyclable cans to fill both bags. On good days, he sometimes gathered enough to buy diapers for his son and gas for the car.

As he approached the stadium, Ken pulled his hat down further and kept his head low. Green Bay is a small town. Getting laid off was not only financially devastating but emotionally demoralizing as well. His shattered sense of self couldn't handle the additional blow of someone recognizing him.

When Ken went to work in the machine shop of PCMC in February 1980, he figured he was set for life. The company, which built machines for the world's biggest tissue suppliers, was considered by everybody in Green Bay to be one of the best places to work. For Ken it meant a several-dollar-an-hour raise from his mechanic's wages. In fact, in his early years with PCMC, Ken remembers that several paychecks would often pile up atop his dresser, eventually to be cashed when he needed the money. But it was about more than just a good wage. Ken could see that, in a company of this size and stature, there was a lot of opportunity for a smart, enterprising, hardworking guy like him. As a parts delivery person, he was a low man on the totem pole then, but he knew there were many ways to move up. He was confident that a job at PCMC meant he had a secure future.

A year and a half later, Ken was laid off for the first time. His wife was due to deliver their first child any day. "I remember the dread I felt. I had a baby on the way and a wife who had to take unpaid leave from her job to go on bed rest because of premature labor. Our savings were pretty well depleted. How would I replace my income? How would I provide for my new child? The sense of dread and feelings of uncertainty were awful." Four days later, his son was born. "I had really strong feelings of failure and inadequacy, with some periods of depression. We had bought a house but had to sell it and lost all of our down payment money. It was really difficult." Eventually Ken was called back to work, but other layoffs would follow. In fact, in Ken's first six years at PCMC, he never worked longer than eighteen months at a stretch.

In those days PCMC's business was subject to wild swings. The company would receive large orders from customers, then hit a period when it had no work at all. When there was no work, the company laid off low-seniority union members like Ken, as well as engineers and office staff, to cut costs. There was little predictability as to when a layoff might happen. Once Ken found himself working overtime on a Saturday, only to learn on Tuesday that he was being laid off again.

Executive jobs were never touched, and those who held them barely felt the impact of the ups and downs of the business. For people like Ken, those ups and downs often meant financial devastation. There was no way for low-seniority employees to plan for a layoff since there was little communication from the company about when one would happen and how long it might last. If Ken left PCMC, he'd give up the good wages and his chance to grow in seniority in the union. And getting hired by another company during a layoff was next to impossible as many of the other local employers required workers to sign an agreement saying they wouldn't return to PCMC when the downturn was over. It was both a financial and an emotional roller coaster.

PCMC's manufacturing director, Gerry Hickey, was experiencing his own emotional roller coaster. His natural tendency was to be a supportive and trusting leader who gave his team lots of encouragement and helped them solve their problems, but he also gave them plenty of space and freedom to do their jobs. He viewed the people he led as friends. As business pressures mounted, he was given repeated and clear directives to micromanage all activities, including what people were doing on a minute-to-minute basis. This mandate to micromanage took him back to a dark point in his career when at an annual review his supervisor told him explicitly to be tougher on his people, stating, "You need to be a jerk to them. You need to let them know who the boss is!"

Part of Gerry's role was scouting locations outside the United States where the company could move their parts production facilities. His passport was peppered with stamps from countries from Mexico to Poland to China. In essence, Gerry's job was to eliminate jobs in Green Bay and take opportunities away from his friends. With every trip, Gerry felt more demoralized. But he knew that if he stepped aside, his replacement might not do everything that he tried to do for his team of employees. He felt trapped in a sinking ship.

The culture at PCMC grew ever more toxic. The atmosphere was one of fear, insecurity, and distrust. Ken recalls once being asked by company leaders to monitor a friend of his who had just been laid off as she packed up her personal belongings. They wanted to make sure she didn't steal anything on the way out. It made him sick to his stomach. He, like most everyone else, came to work each day wondering if more bad news was imminent. "PCMC had brought in a consulting group to help them decide what to do. They said, 'Here are the people you need to let go to right-size the business.' *Right-size* was the big term at that time. I was a team leader then, and some of my team members were let go without my prior knowledge. There was a day that we refer to as Black Friday. I was walking past my leader's office and one of the people on my team was there, in tears. I had feelings of inadequacy and a sense of failure because I hadn't been told she was being let go. In all, three of my team members were let go that day. I ended up having to go over to their cubicles to console them, help them pack their things and then carry them down to their cars. I felt absolutely terrible."

This story about Ken and Gerry and their company follows a sadly familiar pattern. PCMC had been a market leader but had lost market share to aggressive foreign competition. In its final year as a family-owned business, PCMC lost $25 million on $200 million in revenue. It faced deep uncertainty about the future, experiencing many of the challenges confronting other US-based manufacturing businesses. It responded to its financial difficulties with traditional management tactics like frequent restructurings and layoffs, but succeeded only in exacerbating its problems, damaging its culture, and destroying morale. Fear and distrust were rampant. A corrosive "us vs. them" mentality pervaded the company: union vs. nonunion, office vs. shop, management vs. workers.

Ken recalls what happened when he moved into a nonunion job. "I was offered an opportunity in manufacturing engineering at PCMC.

To use the terminology of the day, I was 'jumping the fence,' going out of the union. The position offered a little bit of hope, an opportunity for some education and growth. But psychologically, it was very difficult because I lost some friends; they stopped talking to me because I was no longer in the union. When I went into the shop to ask questions and get information, some people refused to talk to me." Ken had come to realize that many of his friends saw the union as their foundation, the floor they stood on, their rock. "But I saw the union as a ceiling. There was nothing you could really do to control your own destiny; you were simply a number. No matter how hard I worked, what types of improvements I tried to make, I could never get above a certain grade level that was preassigned."

PCMC moved production of one price-challenged product line to Brazil to access the lower labor costs there. But even that wasn't enough for its largest customer, who laid down an ultimatum: Move primary production to China within three years or we will pull our business from PCMC. The family that had owned PCMC for over eighty years didn't know how to deal with the mounting challenges and essentially gave up. The company had lost money five out of the previous seven years; the outlook for the future of hundreds of team members was bleak.

The solution to their problems wasn't in China, though. It was right in front of their eyes. As Ken recalls, "We knew the business was failing. Some of us knew there were things we could do to help. But it was a very stifling, controlling environment. The leaders in the business who had that control weren't interested in having others engaged in the business. It was a very nerve-wracking and uncertain environment, filled with tension and absolute fear."

—

Everybody Matters is about what happens when ordinary people throw away long-accepted management practices and start operating from their deepest sense of right, with a sense of profound responsibility for the lives entrusted to them. When we say "long-accepted management practices," we're talking about a wide range of behaviors—from how companies treat their team members in meetings to how they handle a multimillion-dollar shock to their bottom line—that begin from the assumption that people are the functions they perform, and that succeeding in business means knowing how to make the hard decisions in the interest of making the numbers. Throughout this book, we're going to tell stories about the many times my company, Barry-Wehmiller, faced a challenge or crisis that could have been answered with sacrificing people for the benefit of the business. Instead, we challenged ourselves with this question: How can we redefine success and measure it by the way we touch the lives of all our people?

At the heart of these stories is a simple, powerful, transformative, and testable idea: Every one of your team members is important and worthy of care. Every one of them is instrumental in the future of your business, and your business should be instrumental in their lives.

This isn't simply idealism, though there's nothing wrong with that. Business leaders are always looking for investments with the potential for good returns, but our focus is on creating value for *all* stakeholders. Machinery can increase productivity in measurable increments, and new processes can create significant efficiencies. However, only *people* can stun you with quantum leaps. Only people can do ten times what even they thought they could. Only people can exceed your wildest dreams, and only people can make you feel great at the end of the day. Everything we consider valuable in life and business begins and ends with people.

We may all know that, yet most of us consistently get these situations all wrong. We apply cruel, myopic solutions. We misjudge the results. Most of these business challenges are not what we think they are.

—

If you drive through many small towns in Wisconsin or Ohio or Michigan, or in rural Pennsylvania or in many parts of California or indeed in most parts of the country, you see sad and stark reminders of a world and a way of life that has gradually ceased to be. Decaying hulks of abandoned factories, shuttered warehouses, and empty office buildings are all that remain of a once-thriving manufacturing economy that delivered secure, well-paying jobs and supported full, vibrant lives for tens of millions of people.

Even among businesses that are still operating, you see numerous companies with a proud heritage that are trying to shrink their way to success, routinely announcing mass layoffs and never-ending "restructurings" in desperate bids to survive. You see people losing their livelihoods, but also their sense of self-worth and hope for the future. You see communities being hollowed out, schools operating at a fraction of their capacity, young people leaving en masse in a despairing search for more meaning and better opportunities elsewhere. It feels like a race to the bottom; everything that can be cut has been cut, and little of value remains.

The cause of all this is a corrosive mind-set that has taken root in the world of business, based on a narrow and cynical view of human beings. The devastation we are seeing today is the predictable end point of an unfolding that started in the first decades of the industrial revolution.

There was a fatal flaw at the heart of the capitalist enterprises that once enabled these communities to flourish: From the beginning, employees were treated as functions or human resources, as interchangeable as the parts they labored to produce. Concessions on safety and more humane working conditions were granted grudgingly and only after protracted battles between uncaring management and militant unions. Lacking heart and passion and soul, such enterprises eventually became easy prey to ever more hard-nosed competitors operating with lower costs and willing to cut every possible corner.

It doesn't have to be this way. It is possible to restore hope and provide secure futures for people living and working in these kinds of communities, indeed in all communities. But to do that, we first have to radically change the way we think about business, about people, and about leadership. If we do so, we can build thriving organizations that bring joy and fulfillment to all who serve them and depend on them.

Though they are the exceptions rather than the rule, organizations do exist today in which everybody connected with the enterprise flourishes: customers, employees, suppliers, communities, and investors. Such companies operate with an innate sense of higher purpose, have a determination to create multiple kinds of value for all of their stakeholders, have leaders who care about their purpose and their people, and have cultures built upon trust and authenticity and genuine caring for human beings.

Most of these "conscious" companies were born that way, and almost all of them operate in growing industries. But there is another less known, but in some ways more compelling, phenomenon that is also stirring. It is a way of being as a business that is slowly bringing about a renaissance in American manufacturing. It is a mind-set that is proving to be effective in diverse locations around the world and that works equally well in business contexts outside of manufacturing. At Barry-Wehmiller, we have evolved a fully fleshed-out business philosophy that we have used to rejuvenate and restore to prosperity dozens of businesses that were floundering, that in many cases were on their deathbeds, so to speak.

This is a story about the power and impact of "truly human" leadership. It is about bringing our deepest sense of right, authentic caring, and high ideals to business. It is about achieving success beyond success, measured in the flourishing of human lives. It is a story of an approach to business and leadership that emerged only in the last twenty years or so in the life of a 130-year-old company, but that has already built a strong track record of enriching the lives of team members and creating extraordinary shareholder value at the same time. It is an approach that has been tested, refined, and proven to work dozens of times in half a dozen very different countries and in numerous towns and cities across the United States.

—

In October 2005, Barry-Wehmiller acquired a struggling PCMC from its then owners, a long-established local family led by a benevolent leader who cared deeply about the organization. But it was also an organization with a top-down approach to leadership, very little trust, and a bit of cronyism. Ken recalls how it felt to work there. "In the period just before the acquisition, I used to stop at a little convenience store for a cup of coffee on my way to work. I had my name badge and entry card clipped to my belt. The young lady at the checkout counter noticed it and said, 'Oh, you work at Paper Converting? That must really suck.' It was surreal and embarrassing to me, because I thought,

'Here is a young lady who is working at a minimum wage job, and she feels sorry for me.'"

As the acquisition was being completed, people in Green Bay were convinced that more production would be moved to lower-cost countries so that the company would be better able to compete, meaning that most of them would have no future with the company. Instead, as a first signal of the new approach, we announced that manufacturing for the product line that had been moved to Brazil would *return* to Green Bay. The news was met with disbelief: Could this possibly be true? Ken felt some stirring of hope. "Within the first week, the Guiding Principles of Leadership (Barry-Wehmiller's vision and values statement) got hung up in the hallway in the office area that I worked in. I remember stopping and looking at it and feeling a sense of hope and yet a sense of doubt. It seemed too good to be true, because in my twenty-five years, this was what everyone wanted but never experienced. I remember thinking to myself, 'Man, if we can do ten percent of what it says in this document, this will be a great place to work.'"

As always after acquisitions, I met with groups of associates that included office, plant, union, and nonunion team members. We told them we would do everything we could to give them a better future and shared a vision of a "great American manufacturing company." I said, "We believe in you. We can turn this business around, and we can do it with the people who are here today. We can compete with equipment made anywhere in the world. Let's go out and build something great together. We will show the world that you can pay people fairly, treat them superbly, manufacture locally, and compete globally—right here in Green Bay, Wisconsin!"

Ken found himself awestruck as he listened. The promise of a new approach to business was encouraging, but he was dubious about yet another management strategy. He remembers, "I wasn't sure what to expect. First we thought that we wouldn't have a job, then we heard about this crazy CEO who was going to focus on fulfillment at work. This guy seemed like he was from another planet."

Sitting next to Ken, a clearly skeptical union team member raised his hand and said, "I want to hear you say that you care about our union." Without missing a beat, I responded, "I don't give a damn about your union . . . I care about *you*."

In the years since, he's come to see I meant it. I believe that if you trust people and show them that you believe in them, they can transform their own lives and the future of a business. Ken remembers the exact moment when he realized this. "We were all wondering when the Barry-Wehmiller people would come in and fix us. I reported to Steve Kemp, who is now the president of PCMC. I asked him when the bus from St. Louis would pull up. He put his hand on my shoulder, and said, 'Kenny, there is no bus. People like you and me, we have to fix this.' Instead of feeling disappointed, I actually felt good; we knew things were broken, but we had ideas, we wanted to try some things, and this gave us a feeling of hope and trust. I felt like somebody finally had faith in me and faith in our ability to improve things."

We promised to create a future for the hundreds of union and non-union team members in Green Bay, so that Ken and many others like him could count on the security of a good job and a fair and predictable wage. We were committed to building a sustainable business model, one that would be resilient in shifting economic times.

Our promise went beyond simply a secure future. I had grown to understand that my responsibility as a CEO transcends business performance and begins with a deep commitment to the lives of those in our care—the very people whose time and talent make the business possible.

We envisioned a new kind of business culture—a culture that puts people first and where true success is measured *by the way we touch the lives of people*. I'm completely obsessed with creating a culture in which all team members can realize their gifts, share those gifts, and go home each day fulfilled. Barry-Wehmiller was already on this cultural transformation journey, and now PCMC would be too.

—

With our guidance, PCMC immediately got busy turning around its broken business. It was clear that they needed to quickly make some changes to restore the faith of their disillusioned, broken-spirited team members. As a first step, we sent a team from PCMC to visit Barry-Wehmiller facilities in Phillips, Wisconsin, and Baltimore, Maryland. These were businesses that were struggling when we acquired them, which we had turned around financially and culturally. Gerry, who was selected to join both trips, recalls his first impression: "Associates in those locations were extremely enthusiastic and involved in the business. We were invited to speak with whomever we wanted to; they had nothing to hide. Rather than being told what to do, the Phillips and Baltimore teams felt engaged in creating their own future, a remarkable contrast from the environment at PCMC, where supervisors micromanaged every activity. Those trips gave us hope that the same thing was possible in Green Bay."

With renewed enthusiasm, the Green Bay team got to work. A clear first priority was expanding PCMC's customer base beyond the industry's few largest companies with their unpredictable buying cycles. The company had become far too reliant on their business and reactive to their needs.

Recall the customer that insisted we move production to China so they could reduce the cost of buying our technology. Our team flew to their corporate headquarters and informed them that PCMC would not be moving production to China. Instead, we gave them our assurance that we would find a way to earn their business while operating in Green Bay. Needless to say, the customer was skeptical. For Gerry, the news lifted an enormous weight off his shoulders. Rather than carrying the guilt of executing a plan to cut jobs, he could now focus on rebuilding his team.

A few months later, senior VPs from that customer were invited back to tour the new PCMC. In the intervening months, the team had worked hard on implementing multiple process changes using the tools of continuous improvement. By examining key processes and making incremental improvement in the ways PCMC executed orders, they were able to get higher-quality parts out in record time. During the visit, the customer group walked around, observing the improvements that had been made and talking to the associates. One senior VP selected an associate from manufacturing who had spent a long time as a member of PCMC's union. He asked, "Does everyone here believe in the change that's happening?" Unprompted, the PCMC associate responded, "No, but we're focusing on those who do believe."

Simultaneously, we made operational adjustments. PCMC's service business was strengthened by introducing a greater sense of urgency and new performance metrics, which resulted in better value to customers and the business. Through it all, the team worked on creating an exciting new vision—an ideal future state—for PCMC. The result? Extraordinary commitment from its hundreds of team members, union and nonunion alike—commitment to being part of the team that would create that better future.

PCMC achieved a healthy turnaround in its first year under our ownership. Within two years, the business started showing financial performance fundamentals that more than validated our faith in its future. The remarkable recovery was overshadowed only by the profound emotional recovery of its team members, who no longer left home for work each morning wondering if the day would bring news of yet another layoff and no longer returned each day drained and dispirited.

Within eight years, we took a company that was losing money, that was near financial insolvency, and that had little hope for the future to a company that has not had any layoffs, has brought jobs back to Green Bay from abroad, is gaining market share, is developing new products, and has become a model of truly human leadership. The transformation at PCMC transcends what can be expressed in numbers. It took real human initiatives to create a culture that today gives people optimism for the future despite the massive challenges they faced. We have shaped an organization over time that has a future in Green Bay with the same team members it had when it was failing. Our unique approach to leadership and strategy has created a business that is thriving!

Gerry Hickey now says that his job as a leader is to see every situation through the eyes of his team. A graduate of every leadership class Barry-Wehmiller University offers, Gerry says that some of his greatest learnings have been to truly understand others, and to listen intensely and work harder on recognizing and celebrating individual accomplishments. Even more importantly, he says the experience has improved his thirty-eight-year marriage to his wife, Wendy. "During the 'dark days' when we were fighting for survival, Wendy would describe me as confused, frustrated, and somewhat bitter. It was impossible not to bring the challenges we were facing home. Now, I think I'm a better listener and a more caring husband, and I think Wendy would agree!"

Eventually, Ken Coppens left his position within the sales administration team to lead continuous-improvement initiatives in two Barry-Wehmiller businesses. Through that role, he discovered his gift to inspire and facilitate change, ultimately leading to his current role as a professor at Barry-Wehmiller University. Today he teaches other Barry-Wehmiller team members around the world courses ranging from Communication Skills Training to continuous improvement to creating a culture of service. His job every day is to inspire change in others, creating a sustainable foundation for Barry-Wehmiller and its culture to endure. That begins with enabling its people to flourish. "Years ago someone dismissed my dream of becoming a teacher, so I did too," Ken shared. "This organization has given me so much opportunity, and I feel this incredible sense of being unchained. It's given me a new life."

—

The Barry-Wehmiller approach to transformation, rejuvenation, and renewed growth has been proven to work in dozens of companies in different industries and diverse cultures around the world. No matter the status of the industry—distressed or vibrant, even companies experiencing severe challenges—our approach has created tremendous stakeholder value. The key pillars are establishing a shared long-term vision, fostering a people-centric culture, developing leaders from within, and sending people home fulfilled.

In the end, it is about truly caring for every precious human being whose life we touch. It is about including everybody, not just the fortunate few or the exceptionally talented. It is about living with an abundance mind-set: an abundance of patience, love, hope, and opportunity.

Everyone wants to contribute. Trust them. Leaders are everywhere.

Find them. Some people are on a mission. Celebrate them. Others wish things were different. Listen to them. Everybody matters. *Show them.* We don't just need a new guide to leading in times of change or adversity. We need a complete rethink, a revolution.

How do I know? Because I started out as one of those leaders who put profits before people, who always thought about costs, never about caring. Eventually, I realized it is all about leadership—but not the kind of leadership I had learned in business school. And that has proven to be more rewarding than any numbers could ever be.

Part One

|The Journey|

Walk with the dreamers, the believers, the courageous, the cheerful, the planners, the doers, the successful people with their heads in the clouds and their feet on the ground. Let their spirit ignite a fire within you to leave this world better than when you found it.

—WILFERD PETERSON

Chapter 1

| The Mantle of Leadership |

My parents were children of the Great Depression—simple Iowa people who came from no money whatsoever, so their families didn't have a lot to lose when everything fell apart. The devastation was felt equally both on the farms and in the cities. My mother, Marjorie Estle, was a farm girl from West Branch, Iowa, who grew up without electricity or indoor plumbing. Often, there was not even enough money for new shoes, let alone extravagances. During high school, she sold tomatoes door-to-door for pennies a pound to earn enough money to buy her first store-bought dress from Lerner's. She was able to go to college only because a kindly banker in town gave her father $500 so he could afford to send her.

My father, Bill Chapman, was a city kid from Cedar Rapids. He and my mother met while they were working in the kitchen of a hospital in Iowa City to help pay their way through the University of Iowa. After he graduated, they got married and moved to Chicago, where my father began his career with Arthur Andersen; they moved to St. Louis when he was asked to help open a new office for the firm. That is where I was born, the middle child of three and the only son.

My childhood was ordinary in every way. I grew up in a three-bedroom ranch house in a middle-class, white-collar neighborhood in Ferguson, Missouri. Because my father worked very hard and traveled a lot, I didn't have much of a relationship with him. I was very close to my mother and to my grandfather; I spent most school vacations happily playing and working at his farm in Iowa. I was an average student in an average high school, never turned on intellectually by my public school education. I rarely read any books that weren't required, and there weren't many of those. My greatest joy was becoming the stage manager for plays and musicals. I designed and built scenery and organized teams to build the sets. If you ask my schoolmates today what they remember most about me, they would likely recall my positive attitude. I was infectiously optimistic and something of a class clown.

After graduating from high school, I started at Cornell College in Iowa but soon transferred to the much larger Indiana University, where I remained an average student. That is when I experienced the first crucible moment in my life: During my sophomore year, my longtime girlfriend and I realized with a shock that she had become pregnant. We were faced with the prospect of becoming parents by the time we turned twenty.

We hurriedly planned a small wedding in St. Louis. I felt like a real loser because I had disappointed everybody. My dad helped us buy a small mobile home. While all my friends were living in dorms or apartments and enjoying a carefree college experience, we lived in a trailer park until I graduated two and a half years later.

I felt a huge sense of responsibility for my wife and child. Almost overnight, I left my irresponsible, underachieving self behind and awakened to a new sense of purpose and focus. I was determined not to let this setback define me or derail me. My life changed dramatically. I worked multiple jobs to contribute to my educational expenses and support my family, and for the first time in my life, I became serious about academics. Everyone who knew me was amazed as I went from being a perennial C student to earning straight As. I graduated with honors with a degree in accounting.

What could have broken me made me. This has been a recurring theme in my life. So many times, I could have admitted defeat, folded my tent, surrendered to fate. But I never did. An indomitable will surfaced time and again; my reaction always was to spring into action, to face challenges head-on, do what needed to be done to extract something positive from every setback.

My father wanted me to get a law degree and become a tax accountant, but I was increasingly fascinated with business and wanted to learn more about it. To me, it was like a sport, with offense and defense, a scoreboard, winning and losing, and all kinds of "game" strategies. I became intensely interested in how businesses create value. So I decided to stay in school and get my MBA from the University of Michigan, one of the top business schools in the country. After graduating, I accepted an offer to work for Price Waterhouse in public accounting, which exposed me to a wide variety of businesses. I was interested in business models, and my role as an auditor gave me a unique vantage point into what made businesses tick. I discovered in myself an ability to look beyond the numbers and clearly see the real issues facing companies.

I didn't notice at the time but realized much later that my business education had ignored the question of how my leadership would impact the lives of other people; instead, it was mostly about how to use people to further my own financial success. I was taught to view people as functions and objects to be used and manipulated to achieve my own goals rather than as full-fledged human beings with hopes, dreams, fears, and aspirations every bit as legitimate as my own. It would take me a long time to open my eyes and heart to all that I couldn't see or feel before.

I n 1969, as I was finishing my second year in public accounting, my father approached me and asked if I would consider joining the company he now owned, Barry-Wehmiller. He had seen me go from being an average student in high school to a star student in business school, passing my CPA exam on my first attempt and doing well at Price Waterhouse. I had matured almost unrecognizably as I overcame my challenges and was now someone he could talk to about business. Our relationship had been completely transformed.

Barry-Wehmiller traces its roots back to the year 1885, when Thomas J. Barry opened a machine shop in St. Louis to produce conveying and transportation equipment for malt houses. In 1899, Barry's brother-in-law and draftsman Alfred Wehmiller joined him and soon invented a revolutionary new kind of pasteurization machine for Anheuser-Busch. This innovation allowed breweries to ship beer outside their hometowns. The Barry-Wehmiller Machinery Company expanded rapidly to meet the needs of the growing beer industry and soon began shipping equipment all over the world. Alfred Wehmiller died in 1917, and the company stagnated without his innovation and leadership. The Prohibition years of 1919–1933 dealt a nearly fatal blow to the company's domestic business, but it was able to survive due to international sales. The subsequent decades saw the company struggle under the family's leadership, unable to develop new products or enter new markets.

While working for Arthur Andersen as a public accountant, my father was assigned to audit the company. Fred Wehmiller, Alfred's son, was running the company at the time and struggling with ongoing financial challenges. His banks required an audit to support loans to the company. Fred was engineering-oriented but couldn't foster the kind of innovation his father had, nor did he possess the leadership skills the business needed. My father had financial experience and was willing to help lead the business, so the company hired him in 1953 as treasurer. My mother couldn't understand why he would leave the security of Arthur Andersen to join this struggling family business.

Market challenges and the limitations of family leadership had resulted in a weak management team, and my father rose quickly in responsibility. In the mid '50s, he was offered an opportunity to invest in the company. He borrowed $30,000 and acquired a small amount of stock. In 1957, Fred Wehmiller passed away, and the family asked my father to become president. They were anxious to sell the company and asked him to find a buyer. There was, however, virtually no interest from outside investors. After this failed attempt, a lender approached my father and offered to loan the company enough money to buy out the Wehmiller family. It would give my father a controlling interest in the company, with 57 percent of the remaining stock. Over the next ten years, as executives retired, the company retired their stock, and our family's share gradually rose into the high 90s.

All that meant was that our family owned nearly 100 percent of a company that was worth close to nothing. The company's already weak financial performance had become further stressed by the debt it took on to buy out the Wehmiller family. My father made attempts to diversify the business, but the small acquisitions he made simply distracted management and added to the financial instability. Within a couple of years, the company was on the verge of bankruptcy. My father sought a strategic investor to save it, but after doing its due diligence, the investor declined and confidently predicted that the company would be bankrupt within thirty days. Somehow, it managed to stay alive, but Barry-Wehmiller remained perpetually in survival mode, with no vitality or vision for how to create a better future.

Somebody My Father Could Trust

Two of the company's officers—the VP of finance and the VP of pro-duction, who had small amounts of stock—had secretly tried to find somebody to buy the company. When my father discovered this, he felt deeply betrayed. His response was to start going to the mail room every morning, where he and his secretary would open every piece of mail that came into the company, looking for evidence of disloyalty. Occa-sionally, his secretary would give him an update on the gossip going around the company. My father simply didn't trust his leadership team anymore, which is why he asked me to consider joining the company. He had no idea what role I would play other than being a family mem-ber he could trust.

Given the permanent state of crisis in the "family business," I had never seriously considered joining it. But I was about to enter my third year in public accounting and repeat my clients. It was getting to be boring working for the same clients year after year, so I was willing to consider it. My mother worried about this new arrangement between my father and me, given our poor relationship in the past. To make it work, he and I developed an understanding that if anything ever both-ered either of us, we would be honest and talk about it right away. As I was not replacing anyone and my dad simply wanted someone he could trust, I entered Barry-Wehmiller with total flexibility to define my role and shape the trajectory of my career.

My dad was only fifty-four when I joined Barry-Wehmiller and appeared healthy, despite having suffered two heart attacks in his for-ties and fifties. However, the company's struggles and dealing with the Wehmiller family had worn on him. When I joined the company, he handed responsibility over to me as quickly as I could handle it. He would say, "Bob, we have a problem in customer service. Would you go fix that?" Other roles he asked me to take on were engineering liaison, managing international license agreements, financial analysis, and becoming VP of finance. I came to understand the interactions between various functions within the business and the challenges of each. The company had been hammered down by decades of financial challenges and dysfunctional leadership, and it suffered from a lack of innovation; it was in dire need of fresh thinking. I enjoyed each new challenge, and given the state of the company, it was relatively easy and quite rewarding to create new approaches in the areas in which I became engaged.

My innate intellectual curiosity and the diversity of the multifunctional experiences I was getting helped me develop rapidly as a leader. I learned firsthand how the various business functions create value and how they are interdependent. My father continued to give me more responsibilities, and I quickly gained confidence as a leader. My enthusiasm and accomplishments gave my dad comfort and a deep sense of fatherly pride.

A pivotal moment in my leadership journey came when my father said to me, "We've got this tool-and-die business that is losing money. Would you go see if you can turn it around? You can try some of the ideas that you have been talking to me about." So I moved from working on projects to running a struggling twelve-person business called Faircraft Manufacturing. Within a few years, I was able to transform it into a growing electronics business by bringing in house the electronic portion of an inspection product line.

One night in October 1975, I had dinner with my parents at a local restaurant. By then, Dad and I had worked together for six years. He was in a good mood and said to me at the end of the dinner, "Bob, I've decided to make you executive vice president. You're already kind of running the company, and your title should reflect that."

I wasn't surprised or overwhelmed by this. What my father did that night was acknowledge what we both knew; it was the logical next step. He was proud of how I had embraced responsibility and excelled in each of my roles in Barry-Wehmiller. By then, I was feeling fairly good about what I had been able to accomplish in this struggling company.

My parents were leaving the next morning to visit our joint-venture operation in Australia. Before leaving for the airport, my mom asked my father to drop something off at the home of a friend from church. But as soon as he reached their house, my father had a heart attack and collapsed and died. He was only sixty years old.

When I got the call that he had died, I was devastated. My father had given his all to the business. He had sacrificed his health and peace of mind dealing with the extreme pressures that came with leading a business that had struggled so hard for so long. He had paid the ultimate price, passing away so young and leaving behind a company that was still in a precarious state.

I had little time to grieve; the business needed my attention. I had just turned thirty and became CEO and chairman of the board immediately, and I threw myself into the challenge. Fortunately, my father had set up a voting trust with me as the successor trustee. This put me in the position of voting 90 percent of the stock. This was a great gift from my father to me and the family. It created a profound sense of responsibility in me to care for the family as he would have wanted me to. I was deeply motivated to make something of the company for the sake of our family and my father's legacy.

When my father died, Barry-Wehmiller had revenues of around $18 million, two or three million dollars of debt, and negative operating income of $477,000. It employed just under four hundred people, with three unions in the production and engineering areas.

A month later, as I was still finding my feet as CEO, the loan officer from our bank came in and told me, "With your dad passing away, we're going to have to ask you to repay our loan."

The Crucible of Leadership

I was still reeling from the shock of my father's sudden death and grappling with my new responsibilities. The news that the bank was pulling our loan was like a kick in the teeth. This was concentrated adversity like I had never experienced before. But, just as I had when my girlfriend became pregnant a decade earlier, I became intensely focused on survival, saying to myself, "I'm not going down." I grabbed hold of the business with both hands, took control financially, cut costs, and brought to bear a single-mindedness and intensity that the company had never experienced before.

The result was that nine months after my father passed away—the company was then already three months into the financial year—Barry-Wehmiller recorded the best year in its history: a profit of $2.2 million on $22 million in sales. We had grown revenues by over 20 percent and taken the company from being a marginal credit risk to paying down our debt and performing at a higher level than ever before.

I was determined to do whatever it took to cut costs and achieve our budget. For example, I went to the production supervisor in the plant and asked him, "How many expeditors do you have?"

He said, "Eight."

I said, "We can only have four."

He said, "No. You don't understand. We need eight."

I responded, "*You* don't understand. I can only afford four. So we can only have four." The human cost of this was something I just didn't think much about. My singular focus was to pay down the debt and make the company profitable.

The good news was that the company paid off its debt and made the most profit in its history. The bad news was that I started to become overconfident at age thirty. The market was improving and sales were growing. The international business was getting stronger, and our one remaining domestic competitor was struggling to survive. Everything I touched seemed to turn to gold. With our improved financial performance and healthy growth, we were able to attract a new group of banks to provide us with financial resources to support our growth.

Our growth was partly driven by market dynamics that were finally changing in our favor. Several states had recently introduced returnable bottle legislation. Our customers were interested in bottle washers again, and we were the only producer of big multimillion-dollar bottle-washing machines. At the same time, Anheuser-Busch and Miller were duking it out in an intense, classic market-share battle, and Pabst and Schlitz and many other smaller competitors were dying. We supplied both Anheuser-Busch and Miller. As a result, we started to rapidly grow our historic business, which had been declining for years.

While we were experiencing unprecedented growth in our traditional markets, I felt that we also needed to invest in new technology. I hired a NASA engineer who had utilized solar energy to heat the space shuttle. With his help, we developed a solar energy system that could heat pasteurizers. Anheuser-Busch bought the first system for its Jacksonville brewery. It became a high-profile project due to the energy crisis the country was experiencing.

My emphasis on building a foundation for growth and accessing new markets and new technology was showing exciting promise. After returnable bottles are washed, they have to be inspected to make sure they are clean and free of defects. Our engineers came up with an idea for a new electronic inspection system to replace human inspectors. Carlsberg Brewery in Denmark bought a prototype system and made plans to equip all their lines. It looked like it was going to be a huge new business for us. We also started an initiative with an Italian company, under a license agreement, to produce and sell their fillers, which were designed to fill and seal bottles for the beverage industry.

Solar pasteurizers, bottle washers, electronic inspection, fillers—each initiative seem to hold great promise for growth. It was exhilarating to lead this nearly hundred-year-old company into a period of dynamic growth in exciting new markets after decades of stagnation. Revenues climbed steeply, from $18 million when my father died to $71 million five years later.

Jim Williams, our senior operations leader at the time, remembers those days vividly. "We didn't have a lot of competition. We had backlogs that went out eighteen months. Customers were coming to us, wanting our machines, and we would tell them they would have to wait in line. It was just glorious for Barry-Wehmiller. We thought this was a growth curve that was going to go right off the graph."

We were hiring people all over the world and had become the talk of St. Louis because of our phenomenal growth. The media, customers, even our banks—it seemed everybody loved us! Our bankers kept saying, "Bob, just be sure you tell us how much money you need so we can support your growth." They made it easy for us to finance our growth—at a time when interest rates were at historic highs.

Those were exciting times. But going from stagnation to rapid growth so quickly can be as challenging in some ways as going the other way. We

had all these big companies that believed in our initiatives and were voting with their dollars. But we had an organization that hadn't grown at
all for decades and was now dealing with extremely rapid growth. It was
an extraordinary change, perhaps one we weren't quite prepared for.

The Reckoning

I was still in my mid-thirties and had become well known in the industry and community for having rejuvenated a stagnant ninety-five-year-
old company that was now experiencing tremendous growth and
developing exciting new technologies. The banks willingly funded our
growth. But while our revenue was growing, these initiatives required
significant investment, and our profitability was not developing as
quickly as I had anticipated. Our debt rose significantly, though this
did not appear to be a problem for our bankers at the time.

If anybody questioned the logic of our many growth initiatives, I
could defend each one on its merits. But when you suddenly have multiple platforms of growth, keeping your feet on the ground can be challenging, and the cumulative risk can become overwhelming. During
the peak of our rapid growth, I had hired a strategy consultant to help
me manage these growth platforms and determine where we could
thoughtfully take our organization. The consultant told me we were
heading for a cliff; however, I was so enamored with each of our growth
initiatives that I rejected that conclusion.

It turned out the consultant was right. In our historic business, we
were selling equipment to the brewing industry at a pace far exceeding
the growth in beer consumption, driven by the ecology movement
(which greatly increased demand for returnable bottles and thus our
bottle washers) and gains in market share by our largest customers

within the industry at the expense of smaller companies. A demand correction soon occurred, and growing breweries started to buy declining breweries instead of new equipment. At the same time, each of our technology-based growth initiatives ran into technical challenges. The solar energy panels started to warp a little bit. The electronic inspection system in Denmark worked well but didn't catch *every* defect, so Carlsberg decided they couldn't use it. The filling system started having performance problems; orders started declining and our warranty and development costs began to escalate.

Our challenges of managing and funding major growth quickly turned into a daily focus on dealing with a sudden reversal of our success. We had to scale back the teams we had put in place to develop these markets. All our growth had been financed through debt, and we had become a significant borrower. We had gone from zero debt to $22 million on which we were paying 22 percent interest, since the prime rate at the time was a staggering 20 percent. The bank loved it and kept saying, "Bob, be sure you tell us what you need, so that when you need it we can be there for you." But the debt was starting to feel uncomfortable to me.

It all added up to a financial tsunami that hit us hard. By 1983, several factors had accumulated: rising warranty costs, inventory write-downs, and costs that were outpacing revenues, which had peaked at $71 million and were on their way down to $55 million. I went to our bankers in October 1983 and said, "My financial team just told me that because of some issues we're having with warranty costs and inventory write-downs, we're going to lose about $3 million."

They said, "Bob, thank you for telling us, we appreciate the heads-up. Just make sure you understand what has happened so you can address it and help us understand. We consider you one of our top clients."

A week later, our CFO came to me and said, "Arthur Andersen found some more inventory and currency issues. It looks like the loss is going be $5 million instead of $3 million." I went back to the bankers and told them. The banker said, "Let me call you back tomorrow."

The same person who a week earlier told me that I was one of the bank's favorite clients called me the next day and said, "We're freezing your line of credit. We want all our money back tomorrow."

I felt betrayed. I am someone who communicates constantly; when we were growing rapidly, our bankers were right by my side, and I kept them fully informed. They never challenged me and made it clear that they were fully supportive and encouraged our growth.

When you're hooked on easy money and suddenly you don't have it, you're not prepared. It's like somebody getting you addicted on dope and then one day saying, "You can't have it anymore." You go into withdrawal. We were in a state of crisis because we didn't know if we could pay our vendors or make payroll the following Friday—a harrowing prospect for any business.

Leaders always need to act decisively and swiftly, especially in times of crisis. When I took over from my father, I was young and believed that I didn't know very much. So I hired smart people and tried to lead by consensus. But the new executives all wanted to go in different directions. When the banks pulled on me this time, I changed. I learned to be decisive and to trust my own judgment, to make the best decisions I could and immediately act upon them.

When you have to live every week on the cash you collect, your priorities become quite simple: You must make sure you have enough to make payroll. Just like men can't imagine what it feels like to give birth to a child, those who haven't experienced it can't possibly imagine what it is like to not know if you can pay people for their work. It was gut-wrenching to think that so many people depended on me and that their livelihoods were now at risk. When our lead bank suddenly froze our line of credit, we immediately contacted another bank where we had $1 million of available credit and kept that cash in a separate account in case we needed it to make payroll. We resolved not to use it for any other purpose.

Living Day to Day

My greatest learning from this period was about the critical importance of good cash discipline. We lived day to day on the cash that came in from collecting receivables from shipments. Our priority for the little cash we had was to first make payroll and then to pay those vendor invoices that would allow us to get the materials we needed for production so we could ship machines and collect more cash.

For nine months, starting in October 1983, the bank basically had a gun to our head, saying, "Pay us back now." The wide publicity we had enjoyed in our community and in our industry now worked against us as every bank in town knew that we had been branded a substandard credit risk. We were considerably past due paying many of our suppliers. It was humiliating, especially after the euphoria of our high-profile growth years. I was having frequent meetings during this time with our attorney about possibly declaring bankruptcy. Our priorities were simple: Somehow, someway, we had to figure out how to survive.

During this intense nine-month period, I called the team together for a Saturday-morning meeting to try to calm everybody down. Many people were leaving the company, and we were letting other people go because we had to shrink our cost structure. The joke was that the elevator only went one way—down. I said, "Why don't we all get a cup of coffee before we start?" Our CFO looked at me and said, "The vendor just repossessed our coffee machine because we haven't paid them in nine months."

Well, I never liked that coffee anyway! I said, "I will run out and get some coffee and be right back."

My positive attitude was key to not letting our circumstances get me down professionally or personally. I shifted into a decisive leadership style that allowed me to deal with the daily crisis of lack of cash. My family never knew the magnitude of the crisis because I didn't bring any of this home with me. I don't even remember ever worrying all that much about the future, though it certainly seemed bleak at times.

Despite all our struggles, we managed to get through that period without missing a single payroll. All of our bankers and vendors got paid—eventually. I learned more in that period without cash than I had ever learned when the banks made borrowing easy.

After nine months of disappointment and rejection as I tried to re-place our debt, a bank out of Chicago offered to structure an asset-based loan for us. I liken it to borrowing money from a guy in an alley with a dark suit and an envelope. It's like having somebody's hand constantly around your neck. But it was better than nothing. I felt new hope that we could avoid bankruptcy and create a future for the company.

However, if I so much as hiccupped, the bank would own the business.

Chapter 2

| Starting the Acquisition Journey |

I have grown to believe that the best strategy in business is a combination of organic growth and strategic acquisitions. But acquisitions can be challenging, and most of them fail to live up to expectations. I was influenced by Chuck Knight, the CEO of Emerson Electric in St. Louis, who had successfully grown his company in mature markets through numerous acquisitions.

In 1984, with the fragile new financing in place and a keen sense that our nearly hundred-year history was largely irrelevant to our future, I went to our finance department and said, "We need to start making acquisitions so we can access markets and technology that can give us a better future."

They looked at me very professionally and said, "Bob, that is a great idea. We only have one problem."

I said "What's that?"

They said, "We have no money. Do you understand that? We have no money."

I looked at them—this was a defining moment for me—and said, "Don't tell me what we can't do. I didn't tell you we needed money. I said we need to do acquisitions." Undeterred by the fact that we had no money, I went looking for companies to buy.

What do you buy when you have no money, not much experience, and little credibility? You buy something nobody else wants. I went to trade shows scouting for acquisitions. My first target was a struggling electronic inspection company in Denver, Colorado. We had looked at it when we had money but passed on it because it was too expensive. The company hadn't done well under its new South African owner. I walked by the booth and said, "Hey, whatever happened to the acquisition? I remember when you guys were for sale."

They said, "Come on in and talk to us. We're for sale again."

So I started negotiating my first acquisition. I went out to Denver to make an offer. Luckily for me, Tony, the executive of the South African firm responsible for selling the company, liked me and thought my offer was reasonable. But another firm had already put in an offer, which the parent company in South Africa preferred. Because Tony liked me, he gave us a chance to match the other bid. We found a way to do that while still getting the return we needed to justify the offer. We bought the business and merged it with our electronics company in Florida. We took two broken companies each with three to four million dollars in sales, put them together, and within three years created a highly profitable $37 million company.

When I took that first acquisition to our board, their confidence in me was low. Even though I controlled the voting stock, I was still very respectful of the board. Bob Lanigan, our senior director, was chairman of Owens-Illinois, the largest glass company in the world. He said, "Our people looked at this and think this is a good fit for you guys. But let me tell you something, Bob. At Owens-Illinois we call this a 'you bet your ass' kind of deal. We're going to support you, but if it fails, it's all over because we have no margin for error."

So Barry-Wehmiller began doing acquisitions where failure meant death. With that as the alternative, we became pretty intensely focused on making our acquisitions work!

The London Windfall

By 1986, we had done several more acquisitions, mostly in England. Our operational intensity was driving improving results, but our historic business was still struggling as the brewing industry consolidated and rationalized capacity. Our English leaders, concerned by our continuing fragile financial performance, came up with a radical idea. They saw an opportunity to take $35 million of our revenue, most of which came from England, and float this group of businesses on the secondary market in London.

It was a huge challenge to create the fundamentals that would make this new company attractive to public investors. But given our experiences with banks and ongoing issues with our new bankers, we felt it was worth the gamble. If it worked, we could use the proceeds to pay off our debt and still have about $2 million in the bank. We would still own the struggling historic business in the United States, which was not part of the public offering.

The prospect sounded like heaven to me. I shifted my attention onto the public-offering process. It seemed preposterous that these small struggling businesses that we had bought could be viewed as valuable when combined, but it was worth a shot. From October 1986 to May 1987, my singular focus was to make sure that this combination of sunrise and sunset businesses, as the investment banker described them, was harvesting every opportunity for creating value and improved quality of earnings.

The IPO took place in May 1987. Instead of the secondary market, we were able to get listed on the main London Stock Exchange. Stunningly, the offering was oversubscribed thirty-five times; people sent in $1.1 billion in cash to buy $28 million worth of stock! I couldn't be-

lieve what had happened. When the board saw this phenomenal success, they said, "We've never seen anything like this. You bought
businesses nobody wanted and thoughtfully put them together; you
amplified the initiatives to make the combination attractive to the market, and amazingly, it really was massively attractive to the market."

Harvard Business School did a case study on the public offering. My
learning from this sequence of experiences was that you can create value
in mature markets by combining intensity and inspiration. We didn't
get to this outcome by traditional thinking; the precariousness of our
financial situation created the motivation for unconventional thinking
and led to an outcome beyond anyone's imagination.

What I had been through from 1975 to 1987—my dad's death;
banks pulling on me; growing the company rapidly and then the collapse of our growth initiatives; the bank's sudden loss of confidence;
growing the business through acquisitions and then engineering a
highly successful public offering—was a phenomenal amount of experience. It had been a trial by fire—a dramatic, at times gut-wrenching
roller coaster ride. We went from the banks not wanting to lend us any
money at any price the day before the public offering to all of a sudden
having $28 million in cash.

It was a time of euphoria, amazement, celebration, and reflection. I
now finally had the opportunity to think and act outside an environment of crisis. I had been shaped by the challenges we had faced. Now
the question in my mind was, "How can we use this money and everything we have learned wisely to position this company for a strong,
secure future?" I had no stomach for any more roller coaster rides.

Seeing Value That Others Couldn't

The traditional course of action after the success of our public offering would have been to use the $28 million of cash we had from the proceeds of the offering to look for businesses with good technology in better markets to support growth. Given the intensity of our experience, since 1983, of living day to day on cash and being viewed as a poor credit risk, I decided to take some time to reflect on my journey and experience since 1975, when my dad died. I knew we had learned a lot during our dramatic growth, traumatic decline, and then the amazing outcome of the public offering. I initiated a series of dialogues with the leadership team, and with the benefit of these rich learning experiences, we designed a vision of the ideal packaging machinery company—one that would have a good balance of markets, products, and technology. I was convinced that this would allow us to avoid the issues of the past.

We looked for companies that were having problems similar to those we had experienced in the 1980s. We were confident we could address their challenges as we had addressed our own. Such companies are easy to find in the capital goods industry, where there were and still are a lot of struggling businesses. Fortunately for us, these were companies that few buyers were interested in, because most people prefer to buy growing companies with strong financials.

Of the seventy-four acquisitions (and counting) we have done since 1987, perhaps sixty were of challenged companies. As we implemented this unique strategy, we brought the same positive attitude that we displayed even in the worst of times and continued to learn as we grew. Now we had the benefit of financial stability. This strategy allowed us to deliver over 16 percent compounded returns to our investors for over sixteen years—a record of value creation that compares favorably with the legendary Berkshire Hathaway during that time period (see chart).

A major key to our success has been that we use unconventional thinking to identify value that conventional thinking cannot recognize or harvest. Anyone can see value in companies with good management,

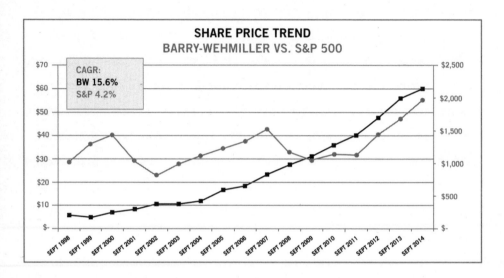

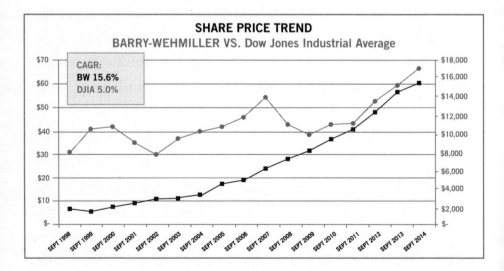

good technology, and good innovation operating in growing markets. We looked for companies where we could create value through our initiatives. We find it deeply fulfilling to take a company that likely would have died and build something vibrant, profitable, and enduring out of it. The unique value drivers that we developed during our crisis years were evolving as we embraced new challenges in each successive acquisition.

Pneumatic Scale was our first target acquisition of significance, with $30 million in revenue. It was a publicly traded company based in Quincy, Massachusetts, near Boston, a hundred-year-old business that started with pneumatic scales weighing food in little grocery stores and evolved to building machines to fill shampoo bottles and the like. In 1989, it was struggling with challenges similar to those we had faced and overcome and experiencing serious financial difficulties. Though the owners weren't interested in selling, I had such confidence that I could help them turn around the business by applying our learning that we bought the company in a hostile takeover, the only time we have done so.

This was the first in a long string of post-IPO acquisitions, every one of them a unique story. We now have ten operating divisions into which we have clustered our acquisitions. We continue to enhance our value drivers and gain more confidence. Our early initiatives where we could consider only very challenged businesses, combined with our financial frailty, sowed the seeds for a unique approach to acquisitions that has evolved over time. According to KPMG, 77 percent of acquisitions fail to achieve their objective. Our record is just the opposite. A few of our acquisitions have not met our expectations, but we have continued to learn and hone our skills with each experience. We are committed to each business we acquire, and *we have never sold a single business in our history*. Combined with our accelerating skills at organic growth, this commitment has allowed us to build an exceptional record for value creation in mature global markets.

The Human Side of Business

At Barry-Wehmiller, I was applying what I had learned in business school, reinforced by what I had experienced in the world of business. When Harvard Business School did a case study on our IPO and I was invited to speak at business schools, my talks were all about strategy and finding value where other people couldn't see it.

At the same time, I was dedicated to being a good father and was striving to learn parenting skills with equal intensity. I had been divorced after twelve years of marriage and three children and had remarried into a "hers, mine, and ours" situation, which brings a unique set of challenges. As my wife, Cynthia, and I brought our families together, we took the responsibility of raising the six kids in our blended family very seriously. I'd go to Young Presidents Organization events where most people talked about market strategies or banking. I was more interested in sessions on how to have a better marriage and be a good parent.

I treated my work and family lives as two separate challenges and didn't see any connection between my commitment to being a good husband and father and being a good leader in business. The human side of my growth was confined to my personal life, where I was working hard to be a good steward of the lives entrusted to me. But at work I continued to view people largely as objects and functions. I considered myself a good person and an optimist, but when it came to business, I was very finance-oriented and totally focused on conventional measures of success: profits, money, and power. I did what I felt I had to do to make money; cut costs, lay people off, shut plants down without worrying about the human consequences. It was, after all, "not personal, only business."

The convergence between the two sides of my life began with another acquisition. In 1997, we bought three businesses with revenues of $110 million from the Bemis Company, easily the largest acquisition in our history. Hayssen was the biggest of the three, with about $55 million in revenues. We saw it as a major opportunity to diversify our business into new forms of packaging with a better future. It would double our revenues from $110 million to $220 million.

Hayssen had a long history in flexible packaging. It had experienced challenges related to global competition and loss of market share, which contributed to poor financial performance. The company had a large base of installed machinery and served a global market. My initial focus was going to be in the customer service area as I felt that an improvement in service could build a foundation for a better future with our existing customers.

On the first day of our ownership, I traveled to South Carolina to see how we could begin to rebuild the business. Around 7:30 in the morning, I was having a cup of coffee, and other people were in the coffee area. I didn't know them and they didn't know me. It was March 1997, and they were talking about March Madness (the national end-of-season college basketball tournament in the United States): which teams had won, how they had bet in the pool, how their "brackets" were doing. They were clearly having a lot of fun, whether they had won five dollars or lost twenty.

I wasn't interested in a specific team or outcome, but I was struck by their body language. They were all highly animated, and the room echoed with raucous laughter. But I noticed that the closer it got to eight o'clock, the more the enthusiasm and joy started to drain out of their bodies. Their shoulders sagged and their faces became serious. They all seemed to deflate a little at the prospect of having to "get to work."

I remember thinking, "This is sad. Why can't work be fun?" We prepare ourselves for years, we get an expensive education, and we are excited to get our first job. But it doesn't take long for the excitement to fade and our job to become "work." People are so joyful, vibrant, and alive when they're having fun. Why can't it be that way when they are working?

I walked down the hallway to the conference room where I was to meet with the customer service team, which was responsible for selling replacement parts and service to our existing customers. We had no agenda; it was just a meeting for us to get to know each other and share some ideas. But my mind lingered on my thoughts as I'd watched those people have fun. Soon after we started, I spontaneously said, "Let's create a game. Whoever sells the most parts each week wins. If the team makes the team goal, the team also wins." I had given this idea no advance thought, and I had never seen this done.

The response was immediate. "Mr. Chapman, you don't understand, that won't work here. You see, we handle different markets. Some of us handle the fresh dairy market, some the snack food market, and so on."

I said, "Well, let's try this. From now on, everybody handles whatever they can and whoever answers the phone can take the order." This was unsettling to them, because it was so different. They came up with objection after objection to convince me that it wouldn't work, but I was able to come up with a good answer for each one.

Despite all their misgivings, we launched the game. There was an individual component and a team component. If you sold the most parts in a week, you got $100. If the team made its goal, everybody on the team got $100. It meant that everybody tried to win, but they also felt good about helping their team win. It was enough money to make it worth winning, but not enough for anyone to lose any sleep over if they fell behind.

Thirteen weeks later—at the end of the first quarter—I sat down with the group again. Sales had gone up by over 20 percent! I asked, "I don't understand. What happened? How did orders increase so much? If somebody calls up and they need a gear, they're not going to buy two. Help me understand."

What they told me was eye-opening, and it became another milestone in my leadership journey. One young man said, "You know, Mr. Chapman, you would think that when we got a big order in the past it was a good thing. We didn't think so."

I said, "Why?"

He said, "Well, when you get a big order, you've got to convert that order into paperwork, you have to do the research . . . it's a lot of work! But now, because of this game, we see every order as a way to win, and we love it."

Another young man said, "We work in customer service. When the phone rings, it's usually somebody demanding something from us or complaining about something we didn't ship or something they needed but we couldn't do. We would keep our head down and try to look busy, hoping that somebody else would pick up the phone. But now, because of the game, we're going down to the switchboard operator and asking how she decides who gets which call. Customers don't get our voice mail anymore; they get our voices, and they are saying, 'Wow! What's going on over there?'"

A young lady said, "Before, when we got something that required engineering input, we'd fill out a form and eventually send it to engineering and eventually they'd get back to us and eventually we'd call the customer back. Now, because we want to make our goal, we walk over to the engineering department and say, 'Can you give me an answer for this right away?' We get back to the customer quicker. They're saying, 'I can't believe how quickly you got back to me.'"

Such conversations with team members provided amazing insights into what would become a key value driver for our business. When people started having fun in their roles, we saw transformation in their customer service skills and growth in the product line. I was getting insights that I never had experienced in management classes or in my leadership journey. The employees were having fun every day, individually and collectively, stretching to meet the challenge of reaching their goal. They knew what the score was every day. It became a game instead of work, and people began to apply their natural skills fully and to thrive.

This simple idea of a game created fun, a sense of purpose and camaraderie. Winning gave people psychological satisfaction as well as recognition and rewards. Hard work and challenges became more rewarding and fun. We saw changes in behavior and in attitude. People liked each other more and helped each other win. They were more joyful, more engaged, and had a stronger sense of achievement.

The typical response when companies have problems in customer service is to bring in a consulting firm to work with team members and teach them how to better serve customers. We didn't give people any training. We just gave them a game, and their natural skills surfaced because they were having fun. They weren't doing what they were told to do; they just naturally did what you would do to win, and guess what happened? Customers were delighted because they were being treated better, getting faster service, quicker answers, and better follow-up.

The doubts lingered for a while. "Well, the problem is that some people might cheat. Say a big order comes in on Friday; if they're already at $100,000, they won't enter it until Monday. That's cheating."

I said, "That's not cheating. That's just intelligent game planning. Let them put it in Monday morning. It doesn't make any difference to the company when they put it in."

People were high-fiving each other; some teams even put up electronic displays so everybody always knew what the score was. Team members started to share their scores, even with their families, who started rooting for them and asking them the score when they came home.

Why do we have scoreboards for sports teams but not for business? Wouldn't it be wonderful if everybody in every job knew at all times what the score was, how they were doing, and how their team was doing? You see basketball players looking up at the scoreboard all the time because they want to know what the score is. If we're behind, we need to do different things than if we're ahead. But in business, we usually have no idea of the impact of our actions. Most people have no idea how they're doing until their annual review, when we give them "constructive" feedback with ten things they could have done better.

This experience showed me that the creative gifts of our people were being suppressed by classic "management" practices. We devised a simple leadership technique that inspired them to share their gifts fully as individuals and as team members. Our learning came from sitting down with them and asking them, "How do you feel about these programs, and how have they changed your approach to what you do?" What people told us was amazing!

We decided to roll this out to another division in Baltimore, where we had an equally dramatic experience. When I walked in, the sign above the entrance said, "Committed to our customers' success." I said to the vice president of customer service, "I'd like to meet with your customer service team. What am I going to find?"

He said, "You're going to find a bunch of pissed-off people."

I said, "I just read the sign over the front door that says, 'Committed to our customers' success.' How could you have a bunch of pissed-off people in a customer service area?"

He then made a classic management statement: *"Well, you know Bob, we probably need to weed a few of them out, but we just haven't had the time."*

I said, "Let me meet with them." Based on our experience in South Carolina, we were fairly confident in the program by now. I sat down with the team, and realized that the VP had understated it. This was a *really* dysfunctional group. It was immediately obvious they didn't like each other and they didn't like their jobs. It was so bad, they couldn't even look at me; they had their heads down.

I said, "Folks, we've learned to play this game. It is good for our customers, and you'll have fun." They had no reaction.

The first week or so was pretty rough as they adjusted to the individual measurements and the rules of the game. People were accusing each other of stealing orders. We had developed some nuances with our incentives; for example, if you sold, say, more than $20,000 a day, you would get an extra $25, just because you did it in one day. One team member had a particularly bad attitude and didn't seem to like her job at all. To make things worse, she had just missed the $20,000 mark several days running. One day she was close again, at $19,000. Out of the blue, one of the other customer service reps said, "Look, I just got this $2,000 order. How about if I let you enter it and you'll have a $20,000 day?" That was transformative for her: that somebody cared for her so that she could win the daily prize, small as it was. With that trigger, and with modest coaching, the team began a transformation from being cynical to enthusiastic. Revenues began to grow significantly, and the culture blossomed.

When people know their goal, they are inspired to express their gifts, and they discover capabilities they didn't even know they had. What we experienced was fun aligned to value creation for the individual, the team, the customer, and the company.

I went back again after the first quarter to the vice president of customer service and said, "What happened? This demotivated team, this culturally challenged team . . . they embraced this game, they helped each other, they're winning, and they're growing sales. What do you think happened?"

I will never forget what he said because this is another classic statement you hear so much in business, another symptom of the sickness of business: *"I didn't think they had it in them."*

I hear this all the time. It's always *them* that's the problem—"they don't get it." What's the real issue? Is it that "they" don't get it, or that leaders don't know how to allow people to express their gifts fully? Leaders never say, "You know, I probably didn't do a great job with my team."

As our team member Matt Whiat puts it, "There is no such thing as an underperforming team, only underperforming leaders. Look for the problem in concentric circles around your desk."

I looked at the VP and said, "You know, they had it in them all along. You just didn't have the leadership skills to allow them to be what they're capable of being." But it wasn't really his fault. After all, he was simply behaving as most managers do and had never been taught how to inspire behavior.

We began to capture what we were learning about inspiring behavior aligned to value creation and applied it to other areas where we sensed opportunities. In each case we saw the same result: People changed dramatically in response to our new approach to inspiring desired behavior, and we created additional value for all our stakeholders.

Chapter 3

| Growing the Human Side|

The experiences we were having opened our eyes to the power of new ways of leading and inspiring people, resulting in profound changes in attitude, performance, and fulfillment. We were amazed at how these simple ideas made people feel and the way they changed behavior. We were inspiring people to fully express their gifts toward value-creating goals, but we hadn't expected that when we started; we simply asked, "Why can't business be fun?" People were showing us that they were capable of things we hadn't imagined. All it took was a different way of leading in which people knew their goals and the score at all times and were inspired as individuals and teams to achieve them.

One of our leaders, Rhonda Spencer, was giving a presentation to a group of investment bankers and talking about how a project we were working on would succeed because our culture was highly collaborative, including sharing of ideas and best practices. One of them asked, "How far does that kind of thinking go in your organization?"

Rhonda said, "Gosh, I don't know." She had grown up professionally in the company and been part of the journey while based in the corporate office in St. Louis. She wondered how people at the front lines of the organization or in a recent acquisition felt about and experienced our culture.

At the same time, I had been thinking about similar things. "There's something bigger going on here. What have we learned from these experiences? How can we build on them?"

I knew that these ideas had generated great business results. But deeper insights had come from a simple question we had started asking people: "How did it make you feel?" What people shared with us in response to that question was astounding and gratifying: their sense of joy, their deep satisfaction at being able to use their gifts fully toward a common vision, their sense of achievement, their pride in sharing their success with their family.

Discovering the Guiding Principles of Leadership

We decided to convene a gathering of twenty thoughtful people to search for the deeper learnings from our experiences. We intuitively felt there was something bigger going on that we needed to understand, articulate, and build on. We identified a cross section of team members from different areas who we believed could reflect on the culture and the business. We sent them some advance readings on leadership and invited them to join the dialogue. Together, we would try to make sense of what we had experienced and learned.

The group assembled in Florida. Rhonda and I talked about what people had told us about how they felt after the games and what it meant to them. Participants started adding their own insights and experiences. We wrote all the ideas down on a board and discussed every word in great detail. Gradually, certain patterns started to emerge. After a day and a half, we stood back and said, "These are guiding principles of leadership. These are the fundamentals of leadership that we should never forget. Everything we do in the future needs to be in harmony with these principles."

Guiding Principles of Leadership

We measure success by the way we touch the lives of people.

A clear and compelling vision, embodied within a sustainable business model, which fosters personal growth

Leadership creates a dynamic environment that:

- Is based on *trust*
- Brings out and *celebrates* the best in each individual
- Allows for teams and individuals to have a *meaningful* role
- Inspires a sense of *pride*
- *Challenges* individuals and teams
- *Liberates* everyone to realize "true success"

Positive, insightful communication empowers individuals and teams along the journey.

Measurables allow individuals and teams to relate their contribution to the realization of the vision.

Treat people *superbly* and compensate them fairly.

Leaders are called to be visionaries, coaches, mentors, teachers, and students.

As your sphere of influence grows, so grows your responsibility for *stewardship* of the Guiding Principles.

We are committed to our employees' personal growth.

barrywehmiller
BUILDING A BETTER WORLD THROUGH BUSINESS

barrywehmiller
bw
betterworld

Our Guiding Principles of Leadership were headlined with the phrase "We measure success by the way we touch the lives of people." That phrase had occurred to me a few weeks earlier when I was trying to craft a tagline for the end of a corporate video we were producing.

The video team had asked me to define what success looked like and suggested that I talk about our growth and profits.

This happened in 2002, soon after Enron declared bankruptcy. The company was blowing up in one of the biggest corporate scandals in history. It had become the embodiment of greed and corruption. Partly because of Enron, the reputation of business leaders had sunk lower than that of lawyers and politicians; in fact, it was the lowest of all professions. I felt embarrassed to be a businessman because of the image created by such companies.

With Enron fresh in my mind, I said to the video crew, "You know, we measure success the wrong way in this country. We measure it by the financial performance and growth of a company, and yet we've got people whose lives are being destroyed every day by the way in which many companies operate. We are going to measure success by the way we touch the lives of people. *All* the people: our team members, our customers, our vendors, our bankers. For every action we take, we need to understand the impact it has on all the people whose lives we touch. If every business did that, the world would be a much better place than it is today."

So I came to our dialogue in Florida with that idea. I said, "Is it as simple as this?" I wrote it on the board as an overarching statement, and the rest of the Guiding Principles of Leadership came from the people in the room that day. When we stood back at the end of the process, I couldn't believe the document this group of thoughtful people had created. They had connected with their deepest selves and natural human instincts; we were overwhelmed with the power and inspirational quality of the thoughts.

"The document we created exemplified how we wanted everyone to treat each other," recalls Maureen Schloskey, a member of the GPL creation team. "We had described a 'perfect culture' that we would all like to aspire to achieve. One of the proudest moments of my life was when I was asked to put my signature on the bottom of the original GPL document."

If we had known how long-lasting that document was going to be and the impact it would have on the organization, we probably would have edited it a little better! But we feel like it needs to exist in its authentic form with grammatical mistakes and all, because that's what we wrote on that day. In all the years since, we've never wanted to change a word. It marked the moment in our company's history when we awakened to who we were meant to be, to our unique purpose in the world. The original document was framed and hangs outside my office at our headquarters.

We came back to St. Louis with the document and sent it out to our senior leaders. Since we hadn't planned to create such a document, we didn't quite know what we were going to do with it. Then Larry Smith, the president of our Thiele division, sent Rhonda a copy of Enron's value statement. It included many stirring phrases like "We do not tolerate abusive or disrespectful treatment. Ruthlessness, callousness, and arrogance don't belong here. We work with customers and prospects openly, honestly, and sincerely."

Soon after, Rhonda challenged me, "Enron had wonderful cultural statements too. How is this not just going to be something that's on the wall?"

That was a stimulus for us to think about what we were going to do with our statement. It was a great document, but what would it ultimately mean for the company? Putting it on the wall wouldn't get it into people's hearts. We could deliver top-down lectures and demand adherence to the written principles, but we would be just as likely to see them ignored. Would people do the right thing, left to their own devices, or did we need to watch them every moment to keep them in line?

I said, "We're going to take it off the wall and get it into people's hearts. We'll do that by asking people what we need to change." So I began having dialogues with groups of team members across the company—union, nonunion, office, plant, men, women, all age groups—and talked about what we believed in. We gave people the document and asked them, "What does this mean to you? What are we doing that doesn't match up to what we say here?"

Our cultural transformation began by building a deep sense of understanding and ownership of that foundational document through those conversations. They proved to be so powerful that, to this day, it's still the way we share the Guiding Principles of Leadership with new hires and newly acquired businesses. One of the first things we do when we acquire a company is share the document with our new team members and talk about what we believe in. It is a way for people in the organization to call to our attention areas where we are falling short and to ask for change or be moved to drive change themselves.

The document reflects our highest ideals and aspirations. We didn't write that day what we thought we already were; we wrote what we believed we should be and could be. Our company is on a never-ending journey toward making that vision a reality. On any given day, some of us may fall short, but we always forgive each other and recommit to our vision of being good stewards of the lives entrusted to us.

A new era in our company's growth and evolution had begun. The human side of our business was beginning to come into focus. My family life and personal values were beginning to migrate in natural ways into our approach to business. The consequences would be profound for me and for the business and all the lives it touched in ways big and small.

Living the Message: "Why Don't You Trust Me?"

To weave the Guiding Principles into the fabric of the organization, we traveled among our business units, sitting down with small groups of team members to discuss the vision, the meaning behind the words, and their feelings about it. I would say, "This is what we believe in. Talk to me about it. How are we doing in terms of leading with these principles?"

Many people talked about what they considered the single most important word in that document: trust. I remember a conversation I had early on with Ron Campbell, a veteran machine tester who had been with the company for twenty-seven years. Ron had just returned from spending three months in Puerto Rico installing equipment for our Hayssen Flexible Systems division. He had a lot to say.

"First of all," Ron asked, "if I tell you the truth, will I still have a job tomorrow?"

I replied, "If you have any trouble about what you say today, give me a call." Believing that I was sincere and truly wanted to know how he felt, Ron opened up.

"Well, I see you have the word 'trust' near the top of this document," he began. "However, it seems like you trust me a lot more when you can't see me than when I'm right here. While I was in Puerto Rico, I was kind of an ambassador of the company, with an expense account and lots of freedom to do my job. I did the work and came back. I walked into the plant Monday morning the same time as a lady who works in accounting. She turned left to go into the office and I went straight ahead into the plant. Just like that, everything changed. All my freedom just slipped away. Suddenly there was all this suspicion and control. It felt like someone had their thumb on me all the time. I had to punch in at a time clock when I walked in, when I left for lunch and when I got back, and when I left to go home. If the lady in accounting wanted to call home to see if her kids made it to school, she could just pick up the phone and call; I had to wait until I had a break and then use a pay phone. If I have a doctor's appointment, I have to get my supervisor to sign off on my card and I get docked for the time; she just goes to her appointment. I had to wait for the break bell to get a cup of coffee or even to use the bathroom. I walk in the same door with engineers, accountants, and other people who work in the office. Why is it that when they go to the office and I go into the plant, we are treated completely differently? You trust them to decide when to get a cup of coffee or call home, but you don't trust me. If you really believe in these Guiding Principles of Leadership, why would you trust me when I was in Puerto Rico and not trust me when I am here?"

When he finished, I said, "That's just the way we've always done it in manufacturing, and no one has stopped to ask why."

"You see," Ron explained, "It's more than just the feeling of not being trusted or the lack of freedom. Sometimes the bell goes off when you're in the middle of something that does not make sense to stop. But the expectation is that you should drop everything and take a break right then. If you keep working and come back from break a little later, people look at you like you're late. And if you skip taking a break to avoid those stares, your coworkers think you're showing them up."

I was moved by his candor and the undeniable truth of what he had shared. These were archaic practices. How could we treat our people, thoughtful responsible adults, with such disrespect and distrust? I told him, "You are absolutely right. Thank you for telling me all this. We are going to change."

I turned to Paul, the personnel leader, and said, "Please take out the time clocks and break bells. Tomorrow." Paul started to offer a number of logical reasons why it could not be done. I told him, "We're going to do this. And we're going to do it across all of our operations." From then on, no matter what door they walk in, our people are treated exactly alike—with the trust and respect they deserve.

I remember our manufacturing supervisor saying, "Oh boy, it is going to be chaos in our plant now!"

I said, "Well, it's very sad you feel that way. Every human being deserves to be treated with dignity and respect."

Soon after that, I walked into a plant with the leader of the business. We walked toward a parts-inventory storeroom that was fully enclosed in a cage. I said to Dan, "What did those people do wrong?"

He said, "What do you mean?"

I said, "Well, I see you have them locked up in a cage."

He said, "No, Bob, they're not locked up. That's the parts area where we secure the inventory."

I said, "Dan, do you really think people are going to walk out of this building at the end of the day stealing shafts and pulleys and screws? Is that really the environment we have?"

He said, "Well, we always secure the inventory. It's the responsible thing to do."

That practice said loudly to our people: "We don't trust you." It reminded me of companies I used to audit where they inspected our briefcases and lunch boxes before we left to make sure we weren't stealing anything. It was humiliating. We began doing away with all such trust-destroying and demeaning practices.

Our eyes were opening to things we had never noticed before. It was all happening because we stated what we believed leadership should be and challenged ourselves to align our practices with those beliefs. The Guiding Principles of Leadership had come off the wall and were getting absorbed into the daily life of our organization.

Mind the Gap

We were learning how to *inspire* people to solve problems rather than trying to manage them out of problems. Insights were coming to me fast and furious because I was constantly having dialogues with people all over the world about what we believed in. My eyes were being opened to numerous traditional practices that were inconsistent with our newly articulated values.

Most businesses believe in their products, value their customers, and use their people to achieve success. We were making it clear to everyone that we believe first and foremost in our people by continually asking them, "What can we do to better align our practices to our Guiding Principles of Leadership?" People came to understand that we truly cared and would not just pay lip service but *really* listen to them. We welcomed everyone's input, and made immediate and tangible changes to align our behavior with the document we had created. We didn't alter the document at all—not one word.

The frequent dialogues with team members were having a deep impact on me. They were challenging much of what I had been taught in my business education and thought I had learned in my leadership journey. It boiled down to this: I was starting to feel a much deeper sense of responsibility for the lives of our team members.

Our business strategies were working well, and we continued to refine them. But now we had entered a new phase of the journey with the awakening of the cultural side. The second and even more powerful engine to power the flight of the organization was coming onstream. We were starting to evolve toward becoming an organization in which people truly matter more than anything else and all leaders recognize the profound impact they have on the lives of those they have the privilege to lead.

Expanding Our Impact Through Acquisitions

Through our success over the past twenty-five years, Barry-Wehmiller has evolved into a company that generates a significant amount of cash every year. After providing a responsible return to our shareholders, we reinvest this cash in the business, both in our existing businesses through activities like R&D and in acquisitions. We acquire businesses where our experience would indicate that we can create value for all stakeholders.

Businesses are acquired all the time—for strategic reasons, because they are unable to survive on their own or because they need assistance and capital in order to execute on growth plans. Frequently, these deals are done by strategic buyers or financial buyers. The focus of financial buyers is typically solely on the financial return. They use financial engineering and an intense focus on wringing out costs to provide a quick profit boost that gives them their return in the shortest time frame. What happens to the business—and its stakeholders—in the long run is not an important consideration. Such transactions are typically about *extracting* value, usually in a zero-sum exchange in which someone else pays the price.

A less common type of acquisition is exemplified by Warren Buffett, who is widely considered a master at *recognizing* value potential. His company Berkshire Hathaway typically buys and holds companies for the long term while leaving leadership teams intact and allowing them to continue operating in the way that made them successful in the first place.

We have taken a very different approach. A few years ago, inspired and emboldened by the success we have experienced at Barry-Wehmiller, we created a separate "hybrid equity" entity called Forsyth Capital Investors, which we charged with a mission to leverage our value-creating experiences outside the confines of the Barry-Wehmiller business platform, which is largely centered on equipment and engineering solutions for industries such as packaging, paper/film converting, and corrugating. Funded entirely by capital from Barry-Wehmiller, Forsyth Capital is now creating new business platforms in multiple areas, starting with printing equipment, insurance services, and medical device equipment. Benefiting from past experience and proven operating and acquisition strategies developed at Barry-Wehmiller, each of these platforms is executing on defined growth plans—organic and acquisition—to become a mini Barry-Wehmiller in its own realm.

This is a patient, purposeful, values-driven approach and it is fundamental to Forsyth's strategy, which can be described as "long-term buy, build, and hold." The typical financial buyer mind-set is "buy and flip," and it focuses only on investor returns. Forsyth aims to create great companies with rich legacies that people can be proud of. It is showing that a more humanistic and holistic approach can generate returns equal to or even greater than those produced by traditional private equity, without using excessive leverage, market timing, mass layoffs, and other typical financial buyer tactics.

Our approach at Barry-Wehmiller and Forsyth is resolutely focused on *building* value rather than extracting value. We have developed the ability to see the potential for value creation where others often overlook it, acquiring challenged businesses far removed from their better days or businesses performing well but not achieving their full potential. In the most despondent enterprises we partner with, we are able to see strengths that have long been dormant but have not been entirely extinguished. The magic key for unlocking their potential lies in getting these businesses to change the way they think about and treat their people. We start by sharing our Guiding Principles of Leadership and letting people know that we believe in them and that we are going to build a better future together.

While we began doing acquisitions in the early 1980s with a very traditional mind-set, our approach has evolved with our embracing the Guiding Principles of Leadership. We now take a more holistic approach with a focus on creating a better future for all the stakeholders in the opportunity. More of an adoption than an acquisition, this way of thinking places far more emphasis on the human side of the transaction and allows us to spread our message in a more powerful way around the world.

Ordinary People Can Do Extraordinary Things

Much of our business culture has fallen prey to the myth that the main driver of progress and profits is finding the right handful of geniuses. Maybe they're MBAs from top business schools or high-profile executives from a competitor, or maybe they're the last people standing from a training gauntlet meant more to weed out employees than actually train them. Our experience is completely different. We've found that a handful of passionate, experienced people can easily outperform any group of so-called stars. All you have to do to unlock their potential is to share a vision of a better future while letting them know they matter, that you value them as full human beings.

You don't need to find "perfect" people. First of all, they don't exist! But the fact is that every person is special; most of us are just unable to see them that way. Ralph Waldo Emerson once said, "If the stars should appear but one night every thousand years how man would marvel and stare." Our culture is one where ordinary people every day do things that amaze and inspire us. People often talk about getting rid of "B players" and replacing them with "A players." Jack Welch practiced a form of this when he mandated that General Electric fire the bottom 10 percent of employees every year and replace them with new people, a practice referred to as "rank and yank." Jim Collins writes of the importance of "getting the right people on the bus." We think it is far more important to have a safe bus and make sure that the person driving the bus—the leader—knows how to take the people to a better place.

It can be quicker and easier to replace people than to develop them. But the sustainable human solution is not to remove from the "bottom" and add to the "top" (which are highly subjective judgments anyway); it is to bring *everybody* up. At a societal level, that is the only workable answer. Business should not be about elites serving other elites; it should be about giving all of our people ways to develop and express their unique gifts. Every person has such gifts; great leaders know how to uncover them.

Of course, there are situations where people are simply not right for the job, but I have found that to be the rare exception. I remember that in 1990, Terry Pendleton, the third baseman for the St. Louis Cardinals, did not play well, hitting just .230. At the end of the year, he got traded to Atlanta. We were happy to see him go, but in 1991 he became the league's Most Valuable Player! Did he change, or was it the impact of different leadership and a different culture?

John Stroup, a board member of Barry-Wehmiller, is CEO of Belden, a public company with revenues of about $2 billion. He marvels at our rather unique approach to people: "If you're leading a big company, you're taught that the most important thing in the world is talent. That usually means hiring the best athletes, the fastest, the strongest, the ones who can jump the highest. That's not been Bob's MO at all. Bob's MO is, 'I'm not about getting the best, I'm about enabling the people I have to be the best they can be.' That completely changes the integration dynamic of an acquisition. If you're taught like I was about getting the best, right after the acquisition you tell thirty percent of the people, 'We don't want you here anymore.' That's a very different cultural experience than 'Hey, welcome! We'd like to help you figure out how you can reach your potential.'"

So many people tell us, "You've got great people and great leaders in this company." But it's all due to understanding that everybody matters. As Simon Sinek, optimist and best-selling author of *Start with Why* and *Leaders Eat Last*, eloquently puts it, "The thing that makes us love our jobs is not the work that we're doing, it's the way we feel when we go there. We feel safe; we feel protected; we feel that someone wants us to achieve more and is giving us the opportunity to prove to them and to ourselves that we can do that. And by the way, it's good for innovation, it's good for progress, and it's good for profit."[1]

I can guarantee you better business results from truly caring about everyone you work with. However, as we'll see, there's a lot more than profits at stake.

Chapter 4

| Leadership Is Stewardship |

I t was a beautiful June day in Aspen, an idyllic setting for an outdoor wedding. My wife and I sat under the tent and watched the father walk his daughter down the aisle. People whispered about how beautiful she looked. I could physically feel the joy they were experiencing. Having by that time walked my own two daughters down the aisle, I deeply related to the emotions my friend was feeling as he spoke the words I've heard many times: "Her mother and I give our daughter to be wed to this young man." He sat down and held his wife's hand with happiness as they watched the marriage take place.

Into my mind came this thought: "I know that's not what he is really thinking. He is thinking, 'Look here, young man. Her mother and I brought this precious child of ours into this world. We've given her all the love and support we could possibly give, and we expect you, through this marriage, to enable her to continue to be everything she was meant to be. We are entrusting you with this sacred obligation. Do you understand that, young man?' "

Isn't that the hope of every father as he sees his daughter getting married? My thoughts went immediately to all the people who work for us around the world—all those precious people whose parents also want them to have the opportunity to discover, develop, share, and be appreciated for their gifts and to live lives of meaning and purpose. I thought to myself, "My God! We have seven thousand people, and *each and every one of them is somebody's precious child.* Don't all the parents of our team members hope and expect us to be responsible stewards of their precious children's lives?"

That further opened my mind to this question: What does it mean to be better stewards of these lives?

—

We have a crisis of leadership in this country and in the world. I was stunned—and as a business leader, ashamed—to see the data on this. In the United States, an estimated 88 percent of the workforce, 130 million people, go home every day feeling that they work for an organization that doesn't listen to or care about them.[1] That is seven out of eight people! These are our mothers and fathers, our brothers and sisters, our sons and daughters; they all have a high probability of working for an organization that doesn't care for them as individuals but instead sees them merely as functions or objects, as means to the success of the organization. We live in a world where the phrase "Thank God it's Friday" has become universally accepted. For most people, work is drudgery, a meaningless ordeal to be endured day in and day out.

When I was growing up in the '60s, they used to show us pictures of paper mills with sludge pouring out and contaminating beautiful clear streams. I wish we had a camera for the souls of people walking out of our offices and factories every day; it would make that sludge look pristine.

We're destroying people and killing our culture because we send people home after treating them as objects and functions, instead of caring about them as human beings. We want them more engaged because we want them more productive. We want more productivity out of them because that creates more profits and that creates a better future for the company, but we don't care about them as people.

The good news is that we have the power to change this and begin healing tomorrow. We just need to engage our heads and our hearts in an approach to leadership that validates the worth of every individual, an approach in which everybody matters. Our responsibility as leaders, be it in business, the military, in government, or in education, is to create an environment where people can discover their gifts, develop their gifts, share their gifts, and be recognized and appreciated for doing so—which creates an opportunity for them to have a more meaningful life, a life of purpose in which they feel valued and get a chance to be what they were brought onto this earth to be.

Leadership is an awesome responsibility for the lives entrusted to you. Those who are entrusted with the opportunity to lead must recognize that leadership is not about the leader's self-interest, but about accountability to something bigger than oneself. People come into this world with gifts and talents, full of possibilities and unrealized potential. Our responsibility as leaders is to help them realize those possibilities by looking for the talents and goodness that exist in them and inspiring them to become what they are meant to be. Leaders are called to help people become what they were put on this earth to be as individuals and as part of a team or community.

At Barry-Wehmiller, we use the word "stewardship" to describe our approach to leadership. To us, stewardship means to truly care, to feel a deep sense of responsibility for the lives we touch through our leadership. Those lives can often appear broken, as people suffer through toxic cultures and abusive leadership. Our aspiration is to heal this brokenness and restore people to their full and joyful humanity. Stewardship implies accountability that goes beyond simple business ethics;

it means acting from our deepest sense of right. Stewardship also implies trust and freedom of choice; we're not forcing or commanding followers, we're inspiring and guiding them. It is not about the exercise of power *over* another; it is an opportunity for service, an opportunity to exercise power *through* and with others in service to the greater good, to the shared vision and purpose of the organization, and to those in it.

People Are Our Purpose

In recent years, there has been growing acceptance of the idea that businesses should have a deeper purpose that goes beyond making profits. For example, the Conscious Capitalism movement cites higher purpose as one of the four key pillars or tenets of a conscious business. But the conventional understanding of this type of higher purpose is that it relates to the business the company is in and typically focuses on the customer needs it meets. For example, Whole Foods Market's purpose is centered around healthy eating, Google is all about organizing the world's information and making it easily accessible and useful, and The Container Store helps you get organized so you can feel more in control and thus happier. While all these companies also take great care of their people, they are businesses that have noble product-related purposes.

At Barry-Wehmiller, our primary purpose is crystal clear to us: *We're in business so that all our team members can have meaningful and fulfilling lives.* We do everything we can to create an environment in which our people can realize their gifts, apply and develop their talents, and feel a genuine sense of fulfillment for their contributions. In other words, Barry-Wehmiller is in business to improve lives. We do that through the building of capital equipment and offering engineering consulting. But that's our what, not our why. It simply provides the vehicle, the economic engine through which we can enrich the lives of our team members.

A useful analogy for these two kinds of purpose—product-related and people-related—is the two engines on a jet plane. Of course the plane will fly best if both engines are operating optimally. The plane is capable of flying on just one engine, just not as far or fast. The key is to have both engines, the product *and* the people, working in harmony with an appropriate focus on both.

The greatest expression of benevolence by corporations should be to care about their people. A couple of years ago, an author told me, "I wrote a book on philanthropy in American corporations. It isn't working very well."

I said, "You know what is sad? So many American businesses destroy lives every day, but we make a lot of money, and then we feel really good when we write a check to the United Way for $1 million. But I believe we are creating the need for the United Way in the first place by destroying the lives of the people who create the wealth that enables us to give. I believe the greatest charity is what we could do at work every day to take care of the people entrusted to us."

Soon after that, I met a gentleman who's been extremely successful in private equity. He heard one of my speeches and flew out to have dinner with me. I asked him, "What do you feel good about in your life?"

He said, "I'm known for my gifts to my alma mater, but what I feel really good about is my minority athletic scholarship program."

I said, "How many people do you support each year through that program?"

He said, "Probably six or eight."

I said, "How many people do your companies employ?"

He said, "Probably a hundred thousand."

I said, "What you're telling me is you feel good about helping six or eight people outside the company, but the hundred thousand people who work for you every day, whose life and joy depend upon the way they're treated, they're just objects for your wealth?"

He had no immediate response. At the end of our three-hour dinner conversation, he said, "I get it. I thought I worked so I could do good. You do good *at* work."

The greatest gift, the greatest charity we can give back to society is to be truly human leaders who treat the people under our leadership with profound respect and care and not as objects for our success and wealth. In other words, we need to see ourselves as stewards of the lives we have been given an opportunity to lead and influence.

That is exactly how I think about parenting.

I believed for a long time that business and parenting were totally separate, but my journey of the '80s and '90s eventually awakened me to the realization that good parenting and good leadership are virtually identical. The parenting skills I learned at home trumped the management skills I was taught in business school and honed early in my career. This led to my realization that traditional "management" was a root cause of many of the problems in business and thus in families, communities, and society.

Truly human leadership means sending people home safe, healthy, and fulfilled. If you are a parent, what do you want for your children? You want them safe. You want them healthy, and you want them fulfilled, and you want them to live lives of meaning and purpose. Good leadership and good parenting are both about taking care of the people entrusted to you. All parents feel a deep sense of responsibility for their children, whether they are natural born, adopted, or come to them through marriage. We should feel the same way about all those we are privileged to lead.

What I am describing is not a paternalistic parent-child relationship between a powerless child and a know-it-all, "let me tell you what to do" parent. It is a mutually respectful and nurturing relationship that sees the well-being and development of the person being led as the leader's paramount obligation. Everyone wants to be valued as someone's precious child, and no adult wants to be treated as a child.

Of course, this is not to suggest that one cannot be an outstanding leader without being a parent. Our point simply is that there are significant similarities between good parenting and good leadership, as we define it. Both are about being good stewards of the lives entrusted to you.

Family Business Versus Business Family

Family businesses are often dysfunctional because their leaders attain positions based on their relationship rather than their competence. Ironically, many family businesses are the least family-like in their cultures. That is because their circle of caring often ends at their bloodline. A more positive and powerful idea is to think of the business as a family. Our friend Roy Spence, author and CEO of The Purpose Institute, believes every workplace should be like a family:

1. Create a business family: Not every company is a family business, but every company can be a business family, with unconditional love, forgiveness, and nurturing.

2. Treat each employee the way you would like your kids to be treated where they work.

3. Build a home, not a just a business: Start by building a home that you as a leader and your team members would want to come home to every day.

4. Be a coach: As a parent or a leader, follow the proven role models for exceptional coaching that result in highly productive, responsible, trustworthy, loyal, and caring children/employees.

5. Build each other to greatness: Encourage and insist that each team member—every member of the family—play to his strengths so that each one has the opportunity to become great at what they are good at. A family that respects each individual's strengths—that celebrates the fact that although we are family we are all different and we have each other's back in terms of our weaknesses—will be a formidable business family.

6. Be patient with those who don't "get it": People may have been abused by other leaders. Give them time and space to heal.

7. Let them grow and then let them go: Let people grow beyond your team if that is what is best for them, just like great parents do with their children. Empower them to become great parents to others.

8. Be authentically human: Break bread together, celebrate together, talk it over together, and mourn together. Be proudly "unprofessional."

Leaders Must Inspire

I was sitting in the pew in our church in St. Louis where Edward Salmon, Jr., my longtime mentor, was the rector. I have long been in awe of Ed's wisdom about how to live a good life. Under Ed's leadership, our church was very strong and well attended. On that Sunday morning, as he did every Sunday, Ed delivered an uplifting and inspiring sermon. He ended, as he always did, with, "May your light so shine."

I remember thinking, "What an incredible gift Ed has, to be able to stand up there every week and inspire us all to be our best selves." As I got up from the service, my mind went to a different place, just as it had at the wedding. I said to my wife, Cynthia, "You know what's amazing? Ed has us for less than an hour a week, but we have seven thousand people under the influence of our leadership for forty hours a week! We have a profoundly greater opportunity than the church to uplift and inspire people and to shape their lives by the way we lead them."

That revelation had a huge impact on my thinking about leadership. It had never occurred to me before: People give us the gift of their time for forty hours a week, and the way we treat them, lead them, and inspire them (or not) profoundly affects their life. I pictured myself and our other leaders on a pulpit every day, every hour, for forty hours a week. It made me realize that business can be the most powerful force for good in the world. *Business can change the world if it fully embraces the responsibility for the lives entrusted to it.* That transformative idea was born as I got out of the pew and left the church that day.

I began to understand the profound impact leadership could have on the lives of the people who join us. Along with the wedding experience, this realization awakened me to a higher sense of responsibility of my leadership and the preciousness of every person who is a part of our organization. From that day forward, I gratefully embraced the awesome responsibility of leadership and vowed to use it to enable each and every one of our people to lead fuller, richer, and more fulfilling lives.

Shining a Light on Goodness

I was at a dinner in Phillips, Wisconsin, in 2005. We had recently created Guiding Principles of Leadership Teams to help align our organization to these principles. One night at dinner with the leaders of our BW Papersystems business in Phillips, Julie Podmolick said to me, "You know, Mr. Chapman, you come up and give these speeches that are inspiring to us all, but then you leave and we kind of gravitate back to management instead of leadership. Do you have any ideas on what we could do to sustain and deepen our commitment to these ideals?"

I was struck by a simple idea. I said, "I'm a car nut. I've got this crazy yellow Chevrolet SSR. Why don't I ship it up here? You can put it outside the plant. Have people nominate their colleagues for their goodness, and then have a committee of their peers pick the winner. We'll surprise them with the car, which they can drive around for a week. Everyone who sees them will know that they have been recognized for their goodness."

Years later, the GPL SSR Award is one of the most meaningful things we do. We now have a number of these unique cars that get shipped around the country and are awarded to people based on how well they embody our Guiding Principles of Leadership. I was talking to a gentleman who had won the SSR and asked him, "How does it feel to be recognized by your peers for your leadership abilities?"

He said, "It's nice to know after thirty-two years that I've made a difference." It is unfortunate that it took us thirty-two years to recognize the qualities of this fine gentleman. But it isn't like that anymore. In today's Barry-Wehmiller, recognition and celebration are pervasive.

As a parent, I learned that if more than 50 percent of your comments aren't positive, you are creating an oppressive environment for your child. I see the same thing at work. One expression that I have heard frequently along this journey is, "I get ten things right and I never hear a word, and I get one thing wrong and I never hear the end of it." It applies to families, at work, in every environment. (See the sidebar " 'Brutal Honesty' Is Still Brutal.")

Recognition and celebration are two of the most powerful tools of leadership: Look for the goodness and hold it up and say, "Thank you for sharing your goodness."

This isn't about giving a bonus to someone for being more productive, or giving them a Lucite plaque so that you don't have to give them a bonus. It's about repaying their emotional investment with your own. We give awards to people who achieve something that is important to our culture, not just to our bottom line.

"Brutal Honesty" Is Still Brutal

Some years ago, I was asked to speak at the US Air Force weapons school about leadership. I flew out to Las Vegas, where they train some of the finest pilots in the world. The leaders of the base invited me to dinner the night before I was going to speak. I knew very little about the Air Force or the military, so they explained to me what they did there and how they did it. They told me about "brutal honesty," a practice they were clearly very proud of. The tradition started in the early days of the Air Force; after each mission, people go into a debriefing room to tell the pilot everything he could have done better. They hold nothing back and criticize every single thing the pilot may have done less than perfectly. The intent, of course, is to create the finest flying force in the world to defend our freedom.

I decided to ask a naïve question. I said to the most articulate of the officers, "If that airman was your son, would you talk to him that way?"

Without hesitating, he replied, "No."

I said, "Well, that's somebody's son you're talking to." The room went quiet. Finally, I said, "I'm just curious. If one of your airmen goes out and flies a mission tomorrow and nails it, gets every single thing right, when he comes back to that debriefing room, would you say 'great job' "?

There was another period of silence. One of the officers finally said, "We don't have time to tell them what they did right."

I said, "I don't agree. It is oppressive in any environment if all you talk about is the negative."

A young officer stopped me as I was leaving. He had just realized that he had unwittingly taken "brutal honesty" home and was constantly critical of his young son. He said to me, with tears welling up, "Tonight when I go home, I'm going to tell my eight-year-old son everything I like about him."

At the time, we didn't fully realize that much of the power of the SSR program came from the fact that people sat down and wrote about the goodness of their colleagues. Even though we only pick one winner, fifty to seventy-five people may be nominated for their goodness. Nominees are interviewed, and we write a note that goes home to their families about their goodness. Winners are publicly celebrated. In our culture now, people in the organization are always thinking about the goodness of their colleagues instead of gossiping about their flaws.

The winners say, "I can't believe I got nominated, and I can't believe I won." The first thing they do is call their spouse. If you listen to these calls as many times as I have, you realize what they are really saying: "You know, you are really lucky to be married to me! I was just picked out of four hundred and fifty people as an outstanding leader."

The second thing that people do is take that car over to show to the most meaningful person in their life—their mother. They just want her to know "Mom, I turned out OK."

Leadership Is Caring, Inspiring, and Celebrating

With these awakenings, our cultural consciousness moved into a higher orbit. We had started with a simple idea: "Why can't business be fun?" From that, we saw people express their gifts more fully than we'd ever seen before and experience greater joy. Then it dawned on us that everybody is somebody's precious child. And we realized we could have a greater inspirational impact on people than any other organization if we were good stewards of their lives—after all, we have them forty hours week.

These powerful insights accumulated and soon started to get integrated with our unique business-value-creating strategies. We didn't embrace these ideas because we had a business problem or to make our company more profitable; our business was doing fine. We didn't do it because we wanted to become recognized as the best place to work in America. We did it because our deepest sense of right and responsibility was awakened by these simple but profound insights.

The Health-Care Crisis Is a Crisis of Caring

Did you know that the rate of heart attacks goes up 20 percent on Monday mornings? This sad and startling reality has been confirmed by studies in multiple countries.[2] In fact, heart attacks are only one of several stress-related responses to work. Here is a sad irony of our age: While fewer of us are killed or are subjected to violence of any kind than at any time in human history (Steven Pinker comprehensively documents this in his book *The Better Angels of Our Nature*), more human

lives are being stressed and shortened due to work than ever before. Our work is literally killing us.

Rising health-care costs are a crisis in many countries. The causal chain leading up to that crisis is increasingly clear. The number-one factor in rising health-care costs is the rise in chronic diseases, which account for 75 percent of US health-care costs, afflict 50 percent of adults, and cause seven out of ten deaths each year.[3] The number-one factor in the rise of chronic disease is elevated chronic stress; an estimated 73 percent of Americans have unmanageable stress in their lives.[4] The number-one contributor to heightened stress is work: work that is dehumanizing, work where people feel disrespected and not valued, work that occurs in a climate of politics and gossiping, work where people are under enormous pressure to deliver short-term results at any cost, work where there is an almost total absence of caring and nurturing.

Highly stressful work environments have a profound impact on employees' mental and physical health. Employees working long or odd hours have higher levels of hypertension and work-related injuries. They also have more mental-health problems, engage in substance abuse, and get trapped in unhealthy habits like smoking. Medical bills account for over 60 percent of bankruptcies in the United States. Of course, all of this has a huge impact on the health and well-being of people's families and communities as well.[5]

Corporate leaders everywhere understand the urgent need to act. Wellness programs are booming. The predominant emphasis of these programs has been on lowering costs. But that doesn't work. Instead of focusing on lowering costs, we should focus on increasing caring for the lives entrusted to us. If we do that, costs are likely to decline even further than we expect. Consider Gallup's data on the link between employee engagement and health-care costs: Only 22 percent of US employees are engaged and thriving at work. But the health-care costs for that group are 41 percent lower than for employees who are disengaged, and 62 percent lower than for the 20 percent or so of US employees who hate their work.[6]

So the health-care crisis is really a crisis of caring, and caring starts with leadership. At Barry-Wehmiller, our vision for team member health is "Living well. Thriving together." We inspire our team members to make healthy lifestyle choices so we can all live well and thrive together. Our airwaves are filled with gratitude, appreciation, and recognition. Our organization is thriving, because people know and can feel we truly care about them.

This was the amalgamation of all the things I had learned. My determination to be a good steward of the children I had brought into this world started to extend to all the lives for which I am responsible as a leader. I saw no inconsistency in that. This is why the bulk of our feedback from people who take leadership courses through our internal university is about how it affects their family life. They see that it's about being a good steward of *all* the lives we touch in this world. As one of our leaders puts it, "I can now lead with my heart."

Australian leadership expert Kamal Sarma points out, "There is a myth that warriors make the best leaders. The everyday language of business is filled with warfare terminology: We need to hit the deadline; engage the front line; rally the troops; work with the staff; capture market share."[7] Our approach is extraordinarily successful because we have tapped into something far more fundamental to our true nature, which is the opposite of fear: love. Fred Kofman, author of *Conscious Business*, writes, "Love is strong. It is the most powerful force in the universe. Love is a competitive advantage. Love is abundantly available, and allows for the creation of great value." The most powerful way to create and sustain excellence and fulfillment is to lead in accordance with the human spirit.

What is missing from the world of work is genuine caring for people. *Caring* is a profound word. Our capacity for giving and receiving care is extraordinary, but we routinely shut it down or put severe limits on it. We're taught to turn it off before we walk into the office; instead we're asked to put on our emotional armor. We have become conditioned to view people as functions, and we try to get them to do what we want so we can be successful, not because we care about them. But the human need to care is as powerful a drive as our will to survive. As leaders we should create work environments in which our team members feel safe, cared for, and comfortable being their true, fully human selves.

A recent research report found that "people who worked in a culture where they felt free to express affection, tenderness, caring, and compassion for one another were more satisfied with their jobs, committed to the organization, and accountable for their performance."[8] Expressing emotion should not only be acceptable in the workplace, it should be nurtured and embraced. Showing care, kindness, and compassion for our fellow team members should be as natural as the care we show to our families.

Chapter 5

| Hardwiring Our Culture |

Most corporate cultures are filled with fear, stress, gossip, and politics. As author and *New York Times* columnist Tony Schwartz points out, an environment of fear is deeply toxic to our well-being and our capacity to function well: "The most fundamental, powerful, and enduring fuel for performance is a feeling of safety and trust—in ourselves and in the world around us. . . . Most of us spend the greatest percentage of our waking lives in the workplace. But how much energy and capacity do we squander each day worrying about being criticized by our bosses, in conflict and competition with colleagues, or fielding complaints from clients and customers? As the productivity expert Edward Deming once put it: 'Drive out fear, so that everyone will work more effectively and productively.'"[1]

At Barry-Wehmiller, we have created something extraordinarily rare: a culture almost completely devoid of fear, gossip, and politics. Even our own leaders marvel at this, having experienced very different cultures elsewhere. Here is what Carol O'Neill, who joined us recently as VP of strategy, technology, and key initiatives, said: "One of the wonderful things about Barry-Wehmiller is that it is just not the norm to point out somebody else's weaknesses. That is an amazing cultural difference with other companies. You go to any Barry-Wehmiller facility and you will find that there is a spirit of collaboration and respect for each other. This is true of every interaction. There is none of the stuff that you see in 90 percent of corporate environments, which is that when Jim talks, everybody else rolls their eyes because they don't really respect Jim. There is no politics or gossiping here. Gossip thrives in an organization in which the person at the top is willing to listen to it. But if he or she is not, it doesn't go very far. The person saying something negative about a colleague would feel like an idiot."

Joe Wilhelm, who leads Barry-Wehmiller Design Group, our engineering consulting practice, also marvels at the positive culture we have created: "I've worked with a lot of customers. I've worked for a couple of companies. I can tell you that there is really not a whole lot of politics, if any, in Barry-Wehmiller. The sense of leaders wanting to support other leaders and just doing what's right is simply amazing to me. There are no turf wars, there is no 'stay away from my customers' or 'get out of my space.' In fact, it is the opposite; everyone is always thinking, 'How can I help my colleague do better?' Bob is always focused on positive behavior, and not allowing negative energy to detract from the larger narrative. It's infectious when a leader remains confident and positive all the time. It really doesn't allow for time to dwell on the negative."

Such a culture doesn't just happen by accident. Like most things at Barry-Wehmiller, it is the result of carefully thought out and consistently implemented initiatives.

—

Until 1997—which we mark as the beginning of our cultural journey, the year we realized that work can be fun—we did not pay explicit attention to our culture. After we came up with the idea of using games to create an atmosphere of fun and healthy competition within our customer service and aftermarket sales teams, the next five or six years were marked by a number of new ideas and experiments to begin to define the culture we wanted, and to bring that culture to life in our rapidly growing company. Eventually, we created the Organizational Empowerment team, led by Rhonda Spencer, to oversee our cultural initiatives.

Our cultural growth shifted into a higher gear because of one significant question. We were on a trip and having dinner with a small group; during a lull in the conversation, Brian Wellinghoff, a recently hired team member in the Organizational Empowerment group, startled me by asking, "What is your greatest fear, Bob?"

I'm not one to dwell on fears, so I had to think for a minute. I thought about my church, which had grown dramatically under my mentor, Ed Salmon. When Ed left to become the bishop of South Carolina, the church went into dramatic decline. I saw behavior that I couldn't believe. Our church, which had seemed to be so strong, now seemed to be falling apart, despite the strength of our faith, just because our rector left to pursue a higher calling.

So I said to Brian, very simply but with great feeling, "My greatest concern is that what we develop here won't live beyond my years. We could build something great that is too dependent upon me. If something happened to me, it would fall apart." I intuitively knew that we couldn't keep our cultural journey going if it was "Bob-dependent." It needed to be fully embraced by our leaders now and in the future to be sustainable.

I believe that the ideas that got us started on this journey had come through me, not from me. We needed to create a way for our leadership approach to live on and continue to evolve beyond my time. Like many passionate leaders, I can sometimes come in like a cultural tornado. That stirs things up, gets people inspired, and helps them look at things in a new way. But we realized that in order to build an enduring legacy, we couldn't just rely on a few moments of inspiration.

Rhonda Spencer recalls, "For the Organizational Empowerment team, hearing Bob's response to Brian's question put our role in perspective. How could we ensure that what we were doing was sustainable? What would the legacy of this business be? It clarified what our role should be. We need to be focused on the legacy of this business. Therefore we became much more systematic in what we were doing."

This marked the beginning of a period of intense focus to create discipline and structure around the things we had been doing. No critical part of our business is left to chance, and our evolving culture would not be left to chance either.

Two critical cultural initiatives grew out of the realization that we needed to pursue what we believed in with discipline and purpose: our L^3 journey in 2006, followed by Barry-Wehmiller University in 2008.

Lean and Serene: Continuous Improvement for People

Our first imperative was to find the best ways to have the Guiding Principles of Leadership impact every precious life in our company. Though the company had widely adopted the idea of "measuring success by the way we touch the lives of people," we were still expanding the idea of what success really meant to us. We wanted to move beyond temporary success to lasting significance. But we felt that we couldn't reach lasting significance unless truly human leadership was not just a program or a stated value but a pervasive lived aspect of our culture.

Until this time, our cultural initiatives had been largely aimed at people in sales or customer service. While we had involved people across the organization in discussions around the Guiding Principles of Leadership, and had made many changes on the operational side in response to gaps that were pointed out to us, we felt that we still had not done enough to bring the culture to the 75 percent of our people who worked in operations. We decided that the best way to do that would be to adapt Toyota's well-known Lean methodology for team member empowerment and continuous process improvement—with one critical difference: Virtually all organizations that adopt Lean do so to cut costs and improve profits, but we wanted to use it as a way to spread our people-focused culture more broadly throughout our organization.

We scheduled a kickoff meeting in Green Bay with a group of senior leaders to learn about Lean and begin our continuous-improvement journey. On the first afternoon, a consultant gave an opening presentation on Lean. After forty-five minutes, I stood up and walked out of the room in frustration. The presentation was all about justifying bringing Lean tools into an organization because they help add to the bottom line and get more out of people. The presenter actually said these words, "This will help you get more out of people." That's when I left the room.

Brian followed nervously after me, glancing back to see if the presenter was still speaking. "So, what's going on?"

With fire in my voice, I said, "Brian, we are never going to have a Lean journey like that in our organization. We are not going to suck the life out of people and take advantage of them in that way. We are going to build a Lean culture focused on people or we're not going to do it at all."

I had made it clear that our version of Lean was to be about people. I had studied it enough to know that most companies who begin the journey fail to become Lean companies. I had gone to Boston and met with Jim Womack, who wrote the book *The Machine That Changed the World* and founded the Lean Enterprise Institute. Jim said to me, "Bob,

I can't believe that I wrote this book that's been read around the world, that a huge number of organizations in the country are embracing." Then he said these exact words, "I can't believe it hasn't changed the world."

To me, it was obvious why. Lean has become all about numbers, about waste elimination. Does anyone really believe that team members are inspired by the concept of waste elimination? When people hear that, they worry that *they* might be considered part of the waste that gets eliminated. The real power of what Jim had studied and articulated in his book is that it creates a process for listening to team members and validating their knowledge and ability to contribute. Lean can empower people to take charge of their own work and, by extension, their own lives. It can do more to change the quality of their work lives than almost anything else—provided it is implemented the right way.

I said, "We are not going to go down that path. We are going to go down the path of human thriving." Eventually, we decided to adopt a new name to describe our version of Lean. We call it Living Legacy of Leadership, or L^3: leadership practices so profound that they stand the test of time. L^3 is about engaging people's head, heart, and hands in creating their own future and actively shaping the legacy of the business every day.

We refer to continuous improvement as the gateway drug to engagement and fulfillment. We are probably the only company in the world that began the continuous-improvement journey specifically to bring our people-centered culture to our team members.

—

As we embarked on our journey to bring the ideas of Lean to our organization within our unique culture and beliefs, we quickly hit a roadblock. Our people had been raised in an environment of bosses and supervisors. They had no idea how to lead in this new environment of L^3.

We realized that we needed to define our leadership principles and teach leaders to live them. Beyond simply teaching strategies and tactics, we wanted to create a transformational experience, one that would create lasting personal and organizational change. This became the starting point for the creation of Barry-Wehmiller University, which has become the fulcrum around which our culture revolves and grows. We consider it one of our proudest achievements. Every single course we teach becomes a transformative experience in the lives of those who take it. Most important, every course has an impact on people's personal lives that is usually far more powerful and immediate than the impact it has on their professional lives. We will describe our experience with Barry-Wehmiller University in detail later in the book.

The Ripple Effect of Caring

Back to the Green Bay session with the presidents, the VPs, and the consultant. Craig Compton, our VP of operations for PCMC in Green Bay, had e-mailed me the night before and said, "Bob, sometime tomorrow you may want to go into the plant and talk to this group of people who voluntarily took on a Lean initiative for a big Procter & Gamble project and achieved terrific results. It would be good to acknowledge them and let them tell you about it."

I said, "Why don't you ask them to come to the meeting tomorrow? They can tell everybody."

They walked in the next morning with no knowledge that they were going to be asked to speak in front of all of our presidents and VPs of operations. The team consisted of three people, two union and one nonunion. They talked about how they had come up with ideas to reduce inventory, improve lead time, reduce cost, improve quality, achieve better on-time delivery, and so on—all the usual metrics of Lean. All of these had led to significant performance improvements.

When they were finished, I asked Steve Barlament, a manufacturing team member whom I'd never met before, a question that came to me out of the blue: "Steve, how did it affect your life?"

Now, this gentleman wasn't prepared to walk in and speak in front of all our presidents, and he certainly wasn't ready for the chairman of the company to ask him how it had affected his life. But without missing a beat, he said something that was transformative for me personally and for our whole cultural journey. He said, "My wife now talks to me more."

What's beautiful about this is that it was unrehearsed, it was spontaneous, and it was the truth. He said, "Do you know what it's like, Bob, to work in a place where you show up every morning, you punch a card, you go to your station, you're told what to do, you're not given the tools you need to do what you need to do, you get ten things right and nobody says a word, and you get one thing wrong and you get chewed out? You ask questions and it takes a week to get an answer back. They complain about your salary or your benefits. Do you know what it feels like to go home at night to your family? You feel pretty empty. I used to throw my hat in the door before I'd go in. If it got thrown back out, I'd go down to the bar and have a few beers. If my hat stayed in, I'd go in and see my family. I realize now, in hindsight, that when I wasn't feeling good about myself, I wasn't that nice a person to be around. That was basically every day. But since we began this L^3 program, I've been part of making things better. People ask me what I think; they listen to me, and I actually have a chance to impact things, including my own job. The way we set up the new assembly flow really works, and I can go home feeling that I've done a good day's work, not wasted the day chasing parts or feeling resentful. When I feel respected and know I've done a good day's work, I feel pretty good about myself, and I find when I feel better about myself, I'm nicer to my wife, and you know what's amazing? When I'm nicer to my wife, she talks to me."

When so many people go home each night feeling not valued, it is no surprise that we see so much conflict in families and our communities today. We in business are creating that problem because we see people as objects for our success and not as precious human beings. If we send Steve home feeling better about himself and he therefore has a better relationship with his wife, his kids are going to see the model behavior of their parents, and we're going to raise happier, thriving children. This is how we can start to heal our brokenness: sending people home as better spouses, parents, children, friends, and citizens of their communities.

Today, many businesses have a toxic influence on the well-being of their team members and their families. We lament what is happening to the youth of the world, yet we in business persist in sending people home broken, and there they struggle with their marriages and with parenting. Many business leaders think that people should be grateful and happy simply because they have a job. But the stark fact is that *the way we treat people at work affects the way they feel and how they treat the people in their life*. We subject people to our leadership, good and bad, for forty hours a week, and when they go home, it affects the way they treat others.

Author and business professor Srikumar Rao commented, "I often visit companies that say, 'You know, we really want our employees to do well.' What they mean is, 'We want our employees to do well so they can meet our numbers.' People are treated as mechanisms. It was wonderful to see that the goal here is, 'We want our people to do well at work, and we want them to take this wellness back home into their relationships with their spouse and with their children. We want that because it's good for them and their family; it's the right thing to do.'"

We recently hosted an event for the top sales executives from across the Barry-Wehmiller organization. We had gathered them and their spouses to celebrate their contributions to the organization's success. Before the celebration dinner, we sat down with the group to hear their thoughts on how things were going. The sales executives talked about how much they appreciated our motivation and incentive programs. They were also grateful for our acknowledgment of their contributions. They spoke about our caring culture and the accountability they felt to the organization and to each other.

We then asked their spouses how they felt. Keri, whose husband, John Kasel, joined our Northern Engraving/PCMC subsidiary eleven years ago, shared this: "John's demeanor is completely different than it was with his previous company. You know how it is when you come home in a bad mood. You kick the dog and the dog bites the cat and so on. The ripple effect of an unhappy mood is tremendous. That's how it used to be. Now he comes home happy, more content. And because of that, we are all happier."

This is the ripple effect of caring, the power of emotional contagion. Of course, it's easy to celebrate success when you're successful. The real achievement is remembering your core beliefs when things get hard, and when everyone else is moving in a different direction.

When the Great Recession of 2008–2009 hit, something had to give, and it couldn't be our financial stability as a company. We would have to make sacrifices to survive, and the sacrifices we would make would define us.

Emotional Contagion

Emotional contagion is the unconscious transmission of actions or emotions from one individual to another. People are "walking mood inductors," continuously influencing the judgments and behaviors of others.[2] Elaine Hatfield, the leading scholar in this area, says, "All emotions—joy, fear, sadness and stress—have been shown to be contagious."

Positive as well as negative behavior is contagious, though negative emotions are more contagious than happier emotions. In marriages, which are founded on emotion, having a glum, depressed, or stressed spouse has a strong impact on the other partner.[3]

Some people are more apt to catch emotions than other people, and some people are much better at transmitting their emotions than others. Women are more susceptible to emotional contagion than men, for biological and social reasons. Women are usually better at decoding nonverbal communications and are socialized to be emotionally responsive and expressive.[4]

Emotional contagion is considered by some biologists to be a building block of human interaction, and the effects and consequences of contagion are significant. Yet awareness of contagion is very low. People are not aware of the influence that others' emotions have on their own emotions and behaviors, and often do not realize when the process is happening. When questioned in research studies, few people attribute other people's moods as a factor in their own emotions.[5]

It was once believed that emotional contagion occurs only between individuals interacting with one another. However, studies have now shown that emotional contagion also influences group dynamics, and can lead to improved cooperation, decreased conflict, and enhanced task performance.[6]

Emotional contagion in the workplace is a huge issue. It has to be looked at in terms of positive and negative emotions, and in terms of the interactions between leaders and team members. Sigal Barsade, a leading scholar in this area, notes, "It is important not only that leaders be able to impart their emotions to followers but that they be emotionally attuned to and influenced by their followers, so as to truly understand, empower and lead them. . . . People do not live on emotional islands but, rather, group members experience moods at work, these moods ripple out and, in the process, influence not only other group members' emotions but their group dynamics and individual cognitions, attitudes, and behaviors as well. Thus, emotional contagion, through its direct and indirect influence on employees' and work teams' emotions, judgments, and behaviors, can lead to subtle but important ripple effects in groups and organizations."[7]

There is overwhelming evidence that experiencing and expressing positive emotions and moods tends to enhance performance at the individual level.[8]

There are ways to control contagious behavior. If you are aware of contagious behavior occurring, you can start to control it. An example would be parents telling themselves that their bad interaction with their boss shouldn't affect how they treat their children. In general, however, people are not very good at controlling their emotions and can do so only in spurts.

Chapter 6

| The Test of Our Culture |

Until the 1980s, it was rare for companies to use layoffs to balance the books, or as Simon Sinek puts it, "using people as fodder to make short-term financial results right." In the 1990s, downsizing became a popular word. For public companies, announcements of downsizing are often followed by a jump in the company's share price as investors celebrate these "fat" organizations shedding "unnecessary headcount."

Rightsizing, de-layering, business reengineering, streamlining . . . these are some of the other euphemisms for the now-routine business practice of eliminating jobs to improve profit. Downsizing has become a reflex response to business adversity—like tapping your knee and seeing your leg kick up—to preserve financial performance, raise investor confidence, and boost share price. We know of one company that deliberately over-hires when times are good so it can let people go and get a bump in the share price when it wants to. Another company tries to cushion the blow of layoffs by giving laid-off employees stock options so they can benefit from the stock price surge their departure is likely to trigger.

Simon Sinek puts it this way: "In the military, they give medals to those who are willing to sacrifice themselves so that others may gain. In business, we give bonuses to those that are willing to sacrifice others so that they may gain."

Our society uses a lot of soft words to disguise harsh actions. Once, after giving a speech at an Air Force base, I asked the colonel in charge, "I'm just curious. How do you teach these young men and women to kill people?"

He thought for a minute and said, "Well, we don't teach them to kill people; we teach them to take out targets that made bad decisions."

I said, "Well, I'll be darned. We do the same thing in business. We call it downsizing or layoffs. We don't say, 'We're destroying the lives of fifteen people today.'"

Executives seldom take unconditional responsibility for layoffs. Standard justifications are poor market conditions, mistakes made by the previous management, or some other force out of their control. It would be refreshing to hear a senior executive say, "We really didn't get this right. We made a lot of mistakes in our assumptions about the business and markets, and unfortunately our people are going to have to pay for our mistakes."

You rarely hear leaders talk with compassion about the impact of layoffs on the lives of individuals and their families after companies send them home with damage to their self-worth and a dramatic loss of income. Eighty percent of people report a negative impact on their health within a year of getting laid off, and their risk of dying goes up by 44 percent to 100 percent. The frequency of sickness absences doubles in downsizing companies.[1]

I frequently ask people in various audiences, "How many of you have ever been laid off?" Usually a third of the people raise their hand. I ask, "How did it feel?"

The emotions come pouring out: "It was the worst day of my life. It's such a rejection. I was told to clean out my desk by five o'clock and see the personnel department for my final check. I was told, 'You're gone, we don't need you anymore; we can't afford you anymore.' Then I had to go home and break the news to my family. The shame I felt was almost unbearable. I had to say to them, 'I don't know how we're going to make the mortgage payment, the car payment, pay the college tuition. I don't know what I'm going to do because nobody is hiring.'"

It is even rarer for companies to consider the impact on those who remain in the organization but have witnessed the devastation and shoddy treatment of the people with whom they worked. It is difficult to assess the extent of such "collateral damage." My son Scott was working as a consultant at a firm when they had massive layoffs. He didn't get cut, but many of the people who used to sit near him did. He knew them and their families well and was thoroughly demoralized, as were many others in the company. In such situations, those left behind switch over to survival mode; passion, creativity, optimism, and caring go out the window.

Responding Like a Caring Family Would

All through the mid to late 2000s, Barry-Wehmiller was growing rapidly and profitably. I was out having dialogues about our Guiding Principles of Leadership with people all over the country as well as in Europe. Every time we acquired a new company, I'd sit down with the people and talk about what we believed in and what they could look forward to now that they were part of the Barry-Wehmiller family.

When you talk about something over and over again and you talk about it genuinely, it becomes an integral part of you. These weren't just words anymore to me. Leading up to the 2008–2009 downturn— several years into our Guiding Principles of Leadership, and just after we launched Barry-Wehmiller University—I was feeling it deeply. Our culture was in harmony with who I wanted us to be, with my faith, with my parenting. Everything in my life felt aligned. It was a priceless feeling.

Then we were hit with the worst economic crisis of our lifetime. The news in the financial pages was unremittingly grim; the country and, indeed, much of the world, was engulfed in the worst recession since the Great Depression of the 1930s. The unthinkable was becoming commonplace. Many large financial institutions were on the brink of total collapse, national governments around the world had to bail out massive banks, and stock markets were crashing everywhere. The housing market collapsed like a punctured balloon, and consumer wealth declined by trillions of dollars. By October 2009, the US unemployment rate would reach 10.1 percent, roughly double the pre-crisis level. By then, the average person was working only thirty-three hours a week, fewer than at any time since the government started collecting such data in 1964.[2]

Our company had been through plenty of tough times, of course. But we had never dealt with the kind of external economic conditions that virtually every business now faced. Barry-Wehmiller president Tim Sullivan remembers the time vividly. "The 2008–2009 financial crisis was definitely a very challenging time. For example, in our Baltimore operations of BW Papersystems, we had just come off a year when we were shipping four to six machines a month. The crisis started in September 2008, and by April 2009 we had one machine on our backlog. You just didn't know when it was going to end. There was no question— it was scary. None of us believed that the company would fail, as we had such a solid business model. At the same time, it was a radical departure from business as usual. When you don't have equipment to build, your engineers, your machine shop people, your assembly people don't have anything to work on. The spare parts business kept the machine shop people going to a certain extent. You wonder how you responsibly keep people gainfully employed. Even though we had a solid foundation, you wonder what your responsibility is to your stakeholders. We had banks that expected us to meet financial covenants. So there were some real questions out there."

The carnage ran wide and deep. In 2008, Citicorp laid off 73,000 people, Bank of America 35,000, General Motors 34,000, and Hewlett-Packard 25,000.[3] In January 2009 alone, Fortune 500 companies laid off another 163,662 people.

At our January 2009 board meeting, one of the board members brought up the L word. "Well, I guess you'd better consider doing lay-offs. We need to get our costs in line with these shrinking revenues."

I said, "No, I think we're going to be OK." At that point, our executive team felt that our backlog of orders and prospects was good enough to get us through without impacting our people.

The next month, while visiting our Italian operations, I received an e-mail. PCMC, one of our largest divisions, had a major order put on hold. In fact, several customers were canceling or putting on hold existing large orders—orders against which they had already paid large nonrefundable deposits.

It's one thing not to get new orders because the market is shrinking. But when your backlog (which we thought was going to get us through this) starts evaporating, it's a much bigger blow. It felt like all our customers had stopped doing anything and were hunkered down in survival mode. Our level of concern was rising, and the news from the economy was growing graver by the day. Financial liquidity had nearly dried up; borrowers and lenders were frozen in place, uncertain about where all this was headed. It felt like an irresistible riptide pulling us away from the shore and from safety. When would it stop? When would our feet touch solid ground again? I sat in my hotel room in Italy and thought, "Oh my God, it's going to hit us, and I don't know how hard. What are we going to do?"

We couldn't simply absorb the costs and run the risk of violating our banking covenants. Such a "head in the sand" approach to preserve the status quo could potentially destroy the company's future. We had to find a way to keep our financial results tolerable while keeping the pain to our people at a minimum.

How could we deal with this crisis in a way that was consistent with our leadership vision? Before we had embraced our Guiding Principles of Leadership, when something like this happened we "rightsized" our organization with little hesitation, laying off people in the offices and plants experiencing a significant drop in new orders. It was considered good and responsible management, and I had done it for years. This meant that the burden was primarily carried by the manufacturing team members who were directly engaged in executing orders; senior executives were rarely touched. But our culture and values had changed dramatically along the way due to our continual dialogue about our Guiding Principles of Leadership. If we responded as we had done before, it would seriously damage and potentially destroy the wonderful caring culture we were building. It would render our assertion "We measure success by the way we touch the lives of people" hollow and essentially meaningless.

Beyond the impact on our culture, if we let people go in that brutal economic environment, it would devastate them and their families and even some communities. There were simply no other jobs to be had. Many people would lose their homes, some their marriages. Children would have to drop out of college. The human toll was almost too painful to contemplate.

We simply couldn't inflict that kind of pain on our people. Our vision had given us a moral compass that we didn't have before. It equipped us to face the economic crisis with a much deeper sense of responsibility for the lives in our care. I immediately started thinking about how best to respond to the crisis in a way that was consistent with our vision. I asked myself, "What would a caring family do when faced with such a crisis?" The answer soon came to me: All the family members would absorb some pain so that no member of the family had to experience dramatic loss. Everybody would pitch in with a sense of shared sacrifice and a shared destiny.

So I started crafting ideas. I made a list of natural ways for all of us to take a little pain so that we didn't hurt anyone too much. It came from my heart, which had grown so much in talking about the GPL for all those years. I thought, "What if we implemented a furlough and everyone took a month off without pay? We could also suspend the 401(k) match and do some other smaller things." I e-mailed my leadership team and said, "Let's find a way past this crisis through shared sacrifice. Here are some initial ideas. I'm flying back from Europe soon; by the time I get back, please get the group together and think about how we can accomplish this in a thoughtful, caring way."

Our leaders worked in teams to determine how we could refine and deploy the ideas I had suggested and how we would communicate with our people. Within a couple of days, they had reviewed all the ideas and turned them into actionable plans. What might have been a challenging process became quite simple, given the wide acceptance of the idea of shared sacrifice. It was quite clear to see what the right way to respond would be. Team members throughout the organization would share the burden, even from divisions that weren't badly affected. We decided that team members would take an average of four weeks of unpaid time off. We suspended executive bonuses and the 401(k) match, put in place a reduction in travel expenses, and devised a generous Voluntary Transition Opportunity Program for associates who were close to retirement. I cut my own salary from about $875,000 to $10,500 (which had been my starting salary in 1968 at Price Waterhouse).

By the time I returned to St. Louis three days later, the team was ready. Instead of sending out an e-mail, we decided that the news would be sent out as a video message to the entire organization so that I could communicate with them in as natural a way as possible about what we were planning. Within a week, we deployed a series of initiatives centered on a vision of what a caring family would do. The message was wonderfully well-received. Because it was delivered by video, people felt the authenticity of it; I don't think they would have felt like that without seeing me and hearing the care and concern in my voice.

Here is some of what I said in my communication to the company:

> *We want to share with you an update on our leadership initiatives to address the evolving impact the global economic crisis is having on our business fundamentals. We are not immune to these challenges, but we are intent on shaping our response to be one of shared sacrifice and commitment to our people-centric leadership, which will shape our deliberations and resulting initiatives.*
>
> *You likely recognize that the impact varies widely by division, and what we are going to discuss are the results of a deeply considered thought process as we have struggled to respond to the global crisis. We believe that, to the best of our ability, we have crafted a very measured response that, when fully implemented, will allow us to mitigate the downturn in revenues. We care a great deal about how*

this impacts everyone. We have tried to spread the impact to allow everyone to feel we are all helping each other.

This is a time when our words and actions will truly define our culture, and we hope that over time our team members will appreciate the sincerity of our actions. At Barry-Wehmiller, we strive to "measure success by the way we touch the lives of people." We recognize in the opening statement of our Guiding Principles of Leadership that one of the primary responsibilities of leadership is a sustainable business model. The current economic situation challenges us as leaders to ensure that each of our decisions is in harmony with these fundamental ideas.

To be responsible, we need to maintain a solid financial position that will support a strong relationship with our capital providers. The banking industry is unpredictable as they try to recover from their own traumatic financial situation, which creates a challenge. We need to ensure that our performance supports a healthy relationship that will maintain access to the cash that fuels our future growth and that we utilize in regular operations. Fortunately, we finished FY 2008 in the strongest financial position in our history, and we have a maturity in understanding the dynamics of banking relationships.

Because our executive team had clarity about our shared values and how to respond in accordance with those values, implementation throughout our global organization was quick and smooth. The furlough plan was rolled out within ten days company-wide. Overall, we implemented almost $20 million in cost-saving initiatives and protected everybody's livelihood. To further emphasize our adherence to our Guiding Principles, we said we wouldn't compromise our commitment to education or to our L³ continuous-improvement events. We encouraged team members to use idle time to take classes in our university. We used gaps in the production schedules to accomplish major Lean improvement events. Continuing our signature recognition events, team members found creative ways to make them meaningful without spending a lot of money on the celebrations.

The reaction was astounding—far better than we anticipated. People had been walking on eggshells for months fearing they might lose their jobs. It seemed like everybody around them was getting laid off: relatives, many of their friends, even their pastor. In an instant, the fear that had been spreading like a cancer was gone, replaced with positive feelings of safety, gratitude, and togetherness. The furlough plan affirmed to our team members that we indeed cared about them. They felt an overwhelming sense of relief that they could count on their job and income. There was also a sense of relief that we were acting to preserve the future; prior to our action, some people worried that we might have had our head in the sand, ignoring the realities of the economic crisis. Morale rose dramatically, because people realized they didn't need to worry about their jobs. Most were happy to offer up four weeks of income, knowing that it was not to make the company more profitable but to keep their colleagues from losing their jobs.

We told people, "Take the time off when it works best for you."

Some leaders initially said, "Oh, no, Bob, we have to tell them when they can take time off, because we need to make sure we have enough people to do the work."

But I was adamant about this, saying, "Look, if we're asking them to sacrifice, then we have to give them something in return. We're going to give them the flexibility of when to do it. Just do what you would do if they got sick."

So our team members were able to take the furlough when it was most valuable to them. Some relished being off in the summer with their school-age children; others used the time to do volunteer work.

Some team members stepped forward and "took the time" for colleagues in more straitened financial circumstances who could not afford to lose four weeks' pay. They said, "I can afford to take six weeks off. If somebody can only afford two weeks, I'll take their weeks." Still others needed coaxing to take time away, simply preferring to work through their unpaid time. We insisted that they take the time off and not do any company-related work while they were away. We had people demonstrate incredible caring and a real sense of altruism, helping others simply because they wanted to and expecting nothing in return. In a way, the furlough became a kind of gift to our people, and they responded with generosity and caring.

Bill Ury, a world-renowned negotiator and the author of the classic book *Getting to Yes*, visited some of our operations to experience our culture firsthand. His reaction when he learned about what we had done was: "The idea of taking the furlough, when that came through for people, it was huge! It was a moment of creativity. It was a moment of confidence. People felt a moment of security and realized, 'OK, people really do count in this company!'"

We got through that economic downturn, and the cultural impact was profound. Who you are in your worst of times is not always who you are in the best of times. Your values, beliefs, and culture don't really get tested when times are good. As Simon Sinek put it during one of his several visits to Barry-Wehmiller, "You cannot judge the quality of a company by the good times. You cannot judge the quality of the crew when the seas are calm. We judge the quality of a crew when the seas are rough. The numbers will never come to your aid. Ever. People will. If you feel that everyone is disposable, guess what? They think the same about you. It's reciprocal." Our actions through those toughest of times validated our authentic commitment to the Guiding Principles of Leadership. We witnessed a real coming together in the culture, solidifying us as a company. Rhonda remembers going up to Phillips, Wisconsin, where people had no work during the downturn. She saw people painting lines on the floor who were happier than she had ever seen them.

Our business rebounded after nine months, well ahead of the broader economic recovery. In fact, our fiscal 2010 was a record year in earnings! So we again asked ourselves how we should respond in alignment with our beliefs. I said to Cynthia, "You know, things are getting better sooner than we expected. I wonder what the right thing to do is now, because when it was tough we asked people to sacrifice."

Cynthia said, "Well, why don't you give them a check?"

I thought about it and said, "You know what? They gave up the matching of the 401(k). I'd rather go back and give them the match back because their retirement's important to them and to us." So we overpaid the match until we had fully restored what they had given up. As far as we know, we're the only company in the country to do that. This was a profoundly meaningful action, because our people were resigned to the fact that the money was gone forever. It was another tangible statement that we really do care. It said to our people, "We care that you are saving for your retirement. Thank you for working with us; you helped save the company and save the jobs of your friends."

Looking back, we can see that our shared vision and fierce commitment to measuring success "by the way we touch the lives of people" gave us the creativity, moral clarity, and courage to look for solutions beyond traditional business norms. We recognized that the most fundamental way we touch the lives of our people is by the security of their employment with us, what Sinek calls a "circle of safety." Genuine commitment to truly human leadership means designing a business that offers fulfillment, success, and safety for all stakeholders.

When layoffs occur, the impact on the culture through loss of talent and diminished morale can be devastating. Our experience was just the opposite. Although we had been on a leadership journey centered on our Guiding Principles for more than seven years, many team members still weren't fully convinced of our sincerity. "Walking the talk" during this tough period did more to convey our beliefs, strengthen our culture, and cement our people's loyalty than anything we could verbalize or proclaim through a framed vision statement on a wall.

We had been very vocal about who we are and what we believe in. The downturn challenged all of us as leaders to live up to our own rhetoric. Fortunately, we had laid an important foundation for dealing with the crisis by doing all the work we had done over the years to build trust and collaboration. Across the business, leaders knew each other, understood each other, and trusted each other. When times got tough, there was no recrimination and no finger-pointing, as routinely happens in a "me first" culture.

As I said, we had the best year in our history in 2010. Was it because of how we responded to the Great Recession? I think that response contributed materially. We've had record year after record year financially ever since then. But more importantly, the people who were on the fence about our cultural journey came over. We won a lot of hearts by our behavior and how we stuck to our principles in those difficult times.

Reactions

We were inspired by the resilience of our associates and the overwhelming and consistent desire of individuals throughout the organization to contribute. Especially noteworthy was the fact that even divisions that were not suffering as much (such as the Design Group) were very willing to contribute what they could to spread the impact and allow everyone to feel like one team.

Team members from around the world sent in notes of appreciation, many describing how they had used or would use the time off. Here are some examples:

Dave Gianini, Corporate: I have not personally heard one complaint about our furlough approach to helping save jobs. Our union team members in Green Bay met the target of 1,400 weeks within days of the program announcement on a voluntary, nonseniority basis with full support of the bargaining committee. The 401(k) match suspension was viewed by most team members as a necessary part of the process. Our UAW team members in Green Bay overwhelmingly voted to participate in the suspension, effective June 1.

Amber Frederick, Design Group: Because most of our professionals remain busy as ever, the initiatives are hard to swallow at times, but they do understand our family approach in which everyone gives a little to ensure no one family is devastated.

Mike Kwaterski, PCMC: We presented the [voluntary retirement] plan to the union leadership shortly before it was introduced to the eligible associates, and their response was a pleasant surprise. They commented, "We definitely can see in the plan that the primary focus is toward the retirement decisions of our senior members and not just to force people out the door. When our lawyers looked it over they commented on how unique the options were to each stage of a person's personal situation." Their last comment was truly interesting. The international rep said, "We appreciate PCMC offering this program, which we think is very fair and which we can support. Even if we had had the opportunity to negotiate, we would not have come up with anything better or more well thought out." What better proof that our people-centric philosophy was reflected through the program? The most unique comment that I received was from a gentleman who fit the criteria for accepting the voluntary retirement program perfectly. For most associates it would be a "no brainer" decision to accept it. As I spoke with this individual, he struggled for a full forty-five days contemplating his decision, including consulting with close friends, financial advisers, and even his pastor. He came in to formally decline the program and explained why. He said that everything in his life was in turmoil and uncertainty, including society and the community he lived in, the government, the stock market, his 401(k), and his family life. He then went on to say, "The only two stable things that I can count on in my life at the present time are my religion and PCMC, and I cannot give up either one of those right now." What a statement! It demonstrates how accountable and important each one of us is to all the other 850 associates and families at PCMC and how important it is for us to act responsibly in this economic landscape.

Cheryl Steliga, BW Papersystems: The video communication was great, and one of our manufacturing associates who was actually planning to resign that week and relocate out of the area changed his mind after listening to the video. We are a large company in a small community, and the health of the business is critical to this area. It's not unusual to overhear a conversation in the grocery store or post office about what is going on at BW Papersystems. I've had many associates tell me their friends think they are lucky to work here.

Greg Myer, PneumaticScaleAngelus: All associates have at least one family member, neighbor, friend, or relative negatively affected by the economy. The people affected are not numbers on an unemployment roster; they are people with families to care for, bills to pay, and hopes and plans for the future. On a very personal level, I have seen the pain and devastation that layoffs can bring. My wife was laid off after thirty-one years, along with 400 of her fellow associates. Those layoffs were bad enough, but only a few weeks later an article appeared in the local paper noting that the CEO of her organization was to receive a pay increase bringing his compensation to $15 million! Should anyone wonder why American industry continues to get a black eye regarding its treatment of people? My wife has told many, many people about the Barry-Wehmiller approach to give them hope.

What We Learned

The 2008–2009 global financial crisis was a traumatic experience for most companies. It started out that way for us as well. But because we had our deeply rooted Guiding Principles of Leadership in place, and because we indeed do measure success by the way we touch the lives of people, our way forward became quite clear to us early on. Because of the way we chose to respond, the financial crisis actually ended up being a blessing in disguise for us. It allowed us to cement our culture in a way that very few other things could have done. It took all the people who may have still been on the fence about our cultural transformation off that fence and moved them very squarely into the camp of true believers. Our morale rose, our culture strengthened, and the amount of altruism in our organization increased exponentially.

Too many companies respond myopically and selfishly to crises.

They seek to protect their profits and their executives and sacrifice ordinary team members and their families. George Packer, the American journalist, novelist, and playwright, has written of this corrosive tendency in our society, "There is no sense of shame at the high altitudes of our society. Certain social norms and taboos have disappeared. The idea has gone missing that there are certain things you really shouldn't do, like firing twenty percent of your workforce while giving yourself a big raise as a CEO, which is a very common thing."[4]

We are not running a company to maximize our profits for this quarter or this year or even this decade. We are striving to build an institution that will endure and create value for all stakeholders. Once again, we would like to quote our friend Simon Sinek: "Next time somebody says, 'What are your goals?' stop saying, 'To increase top line revenues by a million dollars or ten million dollars' or whatever you want to do next year. Start saying, 'We're building a company that's going to last one hundred years.' Devote yourself not to firing people, but to giving them an opportunity to contribute, and if they fail, help them up; and if they fail again, help them up again. . . . If you think you are too busy to give time and energy to your people, then they're too busy to give time and energy to you. It is a balanced equation."

One last thought before we move on. Many people find it surprising to learn that truly human leadership was born in industrial America. It strikes them as an odd place for that to happen, a place with unions and factories and machinists and assembly people. But that is where it was born, not in New York City or Silicon Valley. The fact that it was born in an unlikely place is part of its power. We are living proof that it can be done in the most challenging of contexts. It's like that old line Frank Sinatra sang about New York: If you can make it here, you can make it anywhere. If we can make truly human leadership work in these kinds of old-world industrial businesses, then you can certainly make it work in the kinds of businesses that most people nowadays are a part of.

In Part Two of this book, we will explore how this approach to business can be applied by any company in any industry, anywhere in the world.

Part Two

|The Playbook|

Chapter 7

|Envisioning the Ideal Future|

We now turn to the question of how any business can become a truly human business like Barry-Wehmiller. Of course, like all journeys, the Barry-Wehmiller journey has been a very specific one, with its own twists and turns and ups and downs. But there is also an archetypal aspect to this story, just as mythologist Joseph Campbell found with individual transformation stories, which he labeled as "the hero's journey." Is it possible to learn the lessons that have been learned at Barry-Wehmiller over forty years and apply them to other companies with very different histories, cultures, contexts, and leaders?

We strongly believe it is. The approach that Barry-Wehmiller has taken is universally applicable and can be individualized so that every single organization can do this. It doesn't matter if the organization is a business or a nonprofit, private or publicly traded, small or large. As the expression goes, if something exists it must be possible. The Barry-Wehmiller playbook has now been implemented worldwide in close to eighty acquisitions (or, as we prefer to refer to them, adoptions). In the remainder of this book, we will describe this playbook in more operational terms, such that any organization wishing to make this journey can do so. There is no need for anyone to repeat the mistakes of the past, and everyone can benefit from our experience.

The questions we're going to address are: "How can I make it happen in my organization? How can I change my profit-driven, product-focused, management-heavy, low-engagement business into one in which everybody matters, where success is measured by the impact we have on the lives of people, where nearly everyone is a leader and hardly anyone is a manager, where our people are passionate, committed, and inspired every single day, where office politics and petty gossip have given way to truly caring for every person as a precious human being, as well as recognizing and celebrating their innate goodness?"

We believe, and have repeatedly experienced, that if you take care of your people, they will take care of the business. If you genuinely let them know that they matter, they will respond in kind. Trust is the foundation of leadership; if you trust people, they will trust you back. If you engage them in creating a shared vision for the future of the enterprise, and then give them freedom to act in support of that vision, they will do so responsibly, creatively, and enthusiastically. Ordinary people can do extraordinary things if you create the right culture and a sustainable business model. The basics are simple.

The 10 Commandments of Truly Human Leadership

1. Begin every day with a focus on the lives you touch.
2. Know that leadership is the stewardship of the lives entrusted to you.
3. Embrace leadership practices that send people home each day safe, healthy, and fulfilled.
4. Align all actions to an inspirational vision of a better future.
5. Trust is the foundation of all relationships; act accordingly.
6. Look for the goodness in people and recognize and celebrate it daily.
7. Ask no more or less of anyone than you would of your own child.
8. Lead with a clear sense of grounded optimism.
9. Recognize and flex to the uniqueness of everyone.
10. Always measure success by the way you touch the lives of people!

Most people believe things when they see them. We're asking you to accept the premise "I will see it when I believe it." People the world over are hungry for positive change in business and beyond. They are waiting for real leaders to lead. They are eager to share their gifts. Enroll those who get it right away, and be patient and caring with those who are wary. If your commitment to their well-being is authentic and unwavering, they *will* eventually get it, and then they will surpass your wildest expectations.

It doesn't matter how long your business has been around or the challenges you face. Barry-Wehmiller has been around since 1885 and did not undergo its transformation until over a century later. The great thing about business is that despite all the history, all the deeply embedded traditional dysfunctional management practices, and all the baggage of unhealthy relationships and corrosive cultures, it is possible at any moment in time to push the reset button, to embrace a different way of being, and experience dramatic change.

Of course, meaningful change is neither easy nor instantaneous. Truly human leadership is so outside the realm of what most people have been taught and experienced their whole careers. The people you lead are primed; the real resistance is likely to come from your leadership team, who have never been taught this or experienced it. It takes genuine, heartfelt, soul-level commitment from the CEO (as well as from the board of directors in the case of a public company), who must consciously *choose* to lead differently for the right reasons. People are perceptive; they can see *why* you do what you do. Leaders who adopt the language and tactics of truly human leadership simply to get more out of people so they can generate better financial results are wasting their time. We can guarantee that it will not work; doing the *right* things for the *wrong* reasons inevitably leads to unhealthy outcomes. But if you embrace this way of being to help people discover their gifts and talents and to realize their life's purpose, and if you genuinely strive to be a good steward of their lives so they can be good stewards of the lives entrusted to them, you will witness an extraordinary flowering of human potential. This is what drives us at Barry-Wehmiller; our business is not about building machines, it is about building lives. When I am done, I will look back and feel proud of all the lives we touched, not the machines we built.

The best time to transform a culture is when the business is healthy, when there is no crisis and it isn't a matter of life or death—just as people should adopt healthier lifestyles when they aren't already riddled with disease. Unfortunately, human nature is such that it often takes a "burning platform" to get people to take meaningful action. It should never get to that point, but leaders who do find themselves in that situation must move quickly and take measures that can buy time and rekindle hope while longer-term changes can be put into place. Here are some things that have worked well for us in reviving the numerous struggling organizations we have acquired over the years:

1. **Communicate a strong message of hope, patience, and caring**. Struggling businesses are riddled with fear, uncertainty, and doubt. As the leader, it is your responsibility to express grounded optimism, and repeat it as often as you can: "We believe in you, we know how to do this, we have time, and we will help you to create a better future. You are part of the family now, and we will do everything we can to help you realize your potential."

2. **Take immediate tangible actions to "get the patient healthy."** Fix the most compelling problems and remove obvious bottlenecks. You need to see a brighter future and prioritize initiatives to put in place a foundation for that future. Listen to your team, engage them in creating a vision, and give them the responsible freedom to act in ways that will move the company toward the vision.

3. **Start to build teamwork and a sense of oneness.** Break down silos and end dysfunctional practices that pit one part of the business against another. Institute daily "touch meetings" for people to start building relationships and helping everyone start the day on the same page and with a clear understanding of priorities.

4. **Catch people doing things right.** As you begin this journey, make sure you are connected with your teams, listen to them, thoughtfully share your initiatives, and catch them doing things right. Celebrate all progress, even the smallest of steps.

—

Master cellist Pablo Casals was once asked, "How are you able to play the cello with such magnificence?"

He replied, "I hear it before I play it."

Pole-vaulting champion John Uelses relies on a vivid image of winning to spur his performance, and golfer Jack Nicklaus says that vision "gives me a line to the cup just as clearly as if it's been tattooed on my brain. With that feeling, all I have to do is swing the club and let nature take its course."[1]

Recall that in early 2002, twenty team members from throughout the Barry-Wehmiller organization gathered to systematically harness the learnings from our experiences and move the organization's understanding of leadership and inspiration forward. They prepared for the gathering through advance reading assignments, private reflection, and sharing thoughts with each other before they arrived. The team began with a roundtable discussion centered on two themes: What does great leadership look like, and what techniques can we use to inspire people? As the participants deliberated on these questions, it became apparent that something powerful was emerging. At the end of two days, our seminal vision document—the Guiding Principles of Leadership—was born.

The first line in the document—"We measure success by the way we touch the lives of people"—has become our cultural hallmark. The second line is: "A clear and compelling vision, embodied within a sustainable business model, which fosters personal growth." The authors of the GPL articulated an aspiration that extends well beyond simply creating a great place to work. They recognized that ensuring that we have a sustainable business model is essential to the long-run viability of our business and to the lives of our people. We can't be good stewards of the team members in our organization if our business model is flawed.

I summarize this in the phrase "People, Purpose, and Performance." It all starts with our focus on the people whose lives are entrusted to us. Then we rally around a shared purpose to inspire the best in each other and create value through our performance to sustain and evolve our organization.

Why Vision Matters

A vision is like a lighthouse that stands on a rocky shore as a beacon to help guide us safely to where we want to go. An organization's vision paints a clear picture of a compelling, desirable future for everyone in the organization.

Many of us—individuals and businesses alike—drift along from event to event in our lives, reacting to short-term stimuli in ways that we believe further our interests. Our planning horizons tend to be limited to what we can see in front of us; we deal with the current set of urgent priorities so that we can move on to the next set.

Visioning is about asking the big questions: Where are we going?

Why are we going there? How will each of our stakeholders be in a better place when we get there? A good vision sets goals, inspires all team members, and allows leaders to make decisions that move us toward where we are going.

Many consider the purpose of business to be maximizing profits or, in the case of public corporations, maximizing shareholder value. But that is a simplistic idea that, when taken literally, can cause great harm to people and impair the ability of a business to sustainably generate any kind of value, including financial, in the long run. It is *not* the way the leaders of truly great businesses think about their purpose. The purpose of every great business is usually something deeper and more transcendent, aligned with having a positive impact on the world and on the lives of people.

The shareholder value maximization dogma is actually a rather recent phenomenon. As Professor Lynn Stout of Cornell University says, "Shareholder value thinking comes from academics and bureaucrats. It is not required by law, and it's not consistent with the American historical business experience."[2]

Fortunately, there is now growing acceptance of the idea that businesses should have a deeper purpose that goes beyond making profits. For example, the Conscious Capitalism movement cites higher purpose as one of the four key pillars or tenets of a conscious business, along with stakeholder orientation, conscious leadership, and conscious culture.

A clear vision communicates the organization's purpose and values to everyone in the organization. It becomes a touchstone for leaders; every significant decision that they make should be in harmony with the vision. This is particularly important in challenging times, when leaders become tempted to make shortsighted decisions that can run counter to the organization's culture and values. The vision helps team members understand where the organization is headed and feel connected with something bigger than themselves. It can deepen ties with customers, suppliers, and investors.

Every single person in the organization should be aware of the vision and be inspired by it. The vision is encapsulated in a statement that vividly describes what it would look and feel like to achieve the organization's goals. For example, the vision for the Johnson & Johnson unit that designs and makes orthopedic implants is "Restoring the joy of motion." REI's vision is to "Reconnect people with nature," while Southwest Airlines has worked to "Democratize air travel."

Having a vision is not a radical idea. But we have a specific point of view about vision, which is that it should be centered on *people*. Most vision statements relate to a company's products and their impact on customers. We believe that people can be your purpose no matter what product or service you provide. Other companies may measure success by financial outcomes or industry accolades, but we are very clear that we measure success by our impact on our people.

The Virtuous Cycle

Business growth and people growth aren't separate ideas; they are complementary pieces in creating value. We refer to this as our "virtuous cycle."

Companies routinely refer to people as their most important assets. In most cases, what that really means is that they focus on people so that people will produce for them. We believe that we need to succeed *for* our people. To paraphrase Abraham Lincoln, Barry-Wehmiller is a business of the people, for the people, and by the people. That means we constantly look to create opportunities for our people to grow and realize their potential.

Most businesses use people to build products and make money; we use our products to build people. That's why some describe us as an "upside down" company. We are building an organization and a culture in which people can discover their gifts, grow, and thrive. I was once interviewed by a professor of organizational development. After two hours, he exclaimed, "I have never interviewed a CEO who didn't talk about his company's products."

I replied, "We *have* been talking about our products for two hours. It's our people."

Our focus is on our people. But if we could only say that our company's been able to break even every year, you would probably stop reading this book. We're not a nonprofit organization. We have built a company that creates solid financial value. We are a private company but have a market-simulated share price, and we have grown that share price by 16 percent compounded for over twenty years. That is a track record very few companies—public or private—come close to matching.[3]

We owe our people a vibrant future. If we don't create sustainable business value, we can't create a future for our people or give them opportunities to grow. Many people are passionate about designing products; we have greater passion for designing our business model around people. We do it in such a way that no matter what happens externally, our people will have a secure future. Our people need to feel safe, to trust that they can build a career with us, that they can buy cars and houses and send their kids to college and make other important life decisions and commitments with reasonable financial security. We care about performance because we understand that we are the stewards of thousands of lives that are entrusted to us every day—and the much larger number of lives that those people in turn impact.

It's not enough just to be a great place to work; people also want to be part of a winning team. Our success matters to all our stakeholders. Our customers want to know that we will be there to support our equipment for its years of expected life. The communities we touch want to know that we will be able to provide an economic base for the families that call them home. Our suppliers want us to continue to buy from them and help them become better. Finally, our shareholders want to know that we will be a good investment so they can secure their future. If we don't succeed and cease to exist, we lose the opportunity to touch people's lives. We're proud of the great products we build, our excellence in serving our customers, and our record of value creation. Being on a winning team is a big part of the Barry-Wehmiller culture, but *how* we get there is even more important than what we achieve.

Business Visioning and Cultural Visioning

To bring the virtuous cycle to life at Barry-Wehmiller, we do two kinds of visioning: business visioning and cultural visioning. Business visioning is a way to dream about what our business future could be and create a road map that allows us to get there. We start with an eye to the ideal, rather than starting where we are and looking for incremental improvement. We challenge leadership teams to think about what could be possible, not what might go into a three-year financial plan. This is the "what" that we are about.

Cultural visioning is about our "why." It is about values and behaviors: How should we treat each other so we can all go home truly fulfilled? Cultural visioning at Barry-Wehmiller is a disciplined process that has been applied internally in areas such as safety, continuous improvement, and well-being. We have also used it to help develop visions for the Association for Manufacturing Excellence, the Air Mobility Command within the United States Air Force, Our Community LISTENS (a nonprofit primarily funded by the Chapman Family Foundation), and Roquette America, among others.

Let's look at how visioning works at Barry-Wehmiller Design Group, where we first started using visioning in 2001. Design Group provides engineering and technology services for many large companies, including the design and construction of complete manufacturing facilities. It is one of the few businesses that we have built from the ground up instead of acquiring, and it has grown significantly through organic initiatives. Like most consulting organizations, Design Group doesn't have intellectual property or technology patents. In such an organization, it is critical that people come to work every day feeling inspired about what they're doing. From the beginning, the leaders of Design Group were focused on culture, growth, and professional advancement. Concerned that growth and size would damage the culture, they made a conscious decision early on to develop a statement of the culture they aspired to have as they grew. They went through a visioning process that resulted in a document they called "Rules of the Culture."

On the business side, there wasn't a lot of visioning in the firm's first ten years; leaders never paused to ask, "Where are we going?" or "What does next year look like?" It was an opportunistic rather than disciplined approach to shaping the firm's future. Design Group was fueled by the optimism and passion of a few leaders. The only vision was to build something significant that was pure in its intentions to be a truly independent consulting firm that would provide its young engineers with a good future.

A defining moment came in 2001, in the middle of a business-strategy presentation that Design Group Managing Partner Joe Wilhelm was making for me. I stopped Joe in his tracks as he was presenting the following year's budget and a three-year financial plan. Like most organizations, Design Group typically looked at its current performance and targeted a reasonable level of growth on top of that. I challenged Joe to define a vision of what DG *could* be. "Tell me what is possible if your capacity for growth is only limited by your ability to attract exceptional people into a proven business model and a vibrant people-centric culture. What could you be?" It was a crude form of visioning, based simply on DG's capacity to bring great people into the organization.

Joe was a bit apprehensive about answering. Leaders want to deliver on what they say they can do, especially to the CEO of the company. I was asking Joe and his colleagues to step out of their comfort zone and think about what was possible. Joe worried that what he said might morph into his budget and alter the incentive plans of his leadership team.

I asked him to trust me. "I want you to step back and think about what is possible, and how you can do it in a principled way that would be good for our people, would be good for our shareholders, and would provide growth for everyone connected to the company."

At that moment, we moved from conventional "annual budgeting" to the far more powerful leadership tool of imagining what the future could bring. I was never taught visioning in business school and never experienced it in my days of auditing. When we discarded traditional incremental thinking and started exploring together what might be possible, we opened up a new way of thinking and leading. I believe that visioning is the most powerful tool in leadership, essential to being a good steward of the business and its culture. Wilferd Peterson, author of *The Art of Living*, beautifully captures the power of visioning: "Walk with the dreamers, the believers, the courageous, the cheerful, the planners, the doers, the successful people with their heads in the clouds and their feet on the ground. Let their spirit ignite a fire within you to leave this world better than when you found it."

The moment of dramatic change in our thinking was stimulated by our having hired a significant number of professionals to meet the demands of our engagements. We asked ourselves if we could continue to grow at that rate. We studied our fastest growth period and made that our target growth rate for the future. Design Group was a small part of Barry-Wehmiller at the time, and a small player in its industry. We assumed that there was unlimited potential for growth in our markets if we had talented professionals with competitive skills.

Design Group's "Horizon Plan," as it was called, created the opportunity for doubling within five years. We encouraged the leaders to share it with everyone. It became a road map for opening new offices and recruiting additional professionals. Joe wrote a letter to the entire organization, saying, "We have a vision to double the size of the firm in the next five years. We don't know exactly how the journey is going to go, but we have a view of what it could look like." Each leader was asked to make sure that everyone in their office understood what it meant for them.

Joe recalls, "We wanted people to feel inspired, to feel they were part of a growing and thriving organization that had a plan for the future that would impact their lives in a positive way. We want them to feel that there is growth. Where there is growth there is vibrancy and the opportunity for individual fulfillment. People flocked to the vision like a thirsty person drawn to water. They were inspired by it. My role became more of a cheerleader and someone who ensured that the pieces of the vision were in harmony."

Initially, the leaders had some fear of failing, of falling short of the very ambitious goals. I consistently said, "If we fall short of the vision but still experience healthy growth, that's still a positive outcome." I reassured them that there would be no penalty or negative consequence if they fell short. So the Horizon Plan became Design Group's road map, its blueprint for how to run the business. As it turned out, Design Group actually doubled the size of the firm over the next *three* years, and then proceeded to double it twice more in the years following.

Fast-forward to the present. Design Group now does a rolling three-year business-visioning session every year. The 2014 visioning session involved about 135 leaders in the firm in nine different interactive sessions with fifteen to twenty professionals in each group. The sessions are broken up by region and national practice groups. In each session, people step back and ask, "What is possible? What could we be, and how could we achieve it? What type of people do we need to hire? What would it mean to our professionals?" Each group contributes to its own piece of the vision and has full ownership in it. The firm has a concrete plan in place to grow from the current 900 professionals to 2,500 in the coming years.

The business vision has financial implications, but the vision is not driven by that. Joe Wilhelm clarifies, "We use business visioning to create and refine our road map. Throughout the year, we monitor how we're performing against the ideal. We use that to help us decide where we will open up an office, how we will expand our business. When we conduct our visioning sessions, we always start by saying, 'We're never going to compromise our culture. What does this mean for our people? How does this provide opportunities for advancement?' We have never once begun a session nor ended one by asking, 'How are we going to make more money?' It never even enters the equation. We believe strong earnings follow a successful vision when it is implmented with meaning, purpose, discipline, caring, and a strong culture. But if you create a business just with the primary intention of driving profits, then you don't quite know what's going to happen in the future. In fact, it could well have the opposite effect."

The Visioning Process

A good visioning process accomplishes several things. First, it makes the implicit explicit, forcing the organization to articulate its assumptions, beliefs, values, taboos, fears, dreams, and aspirations. Second, visioning helps us paint a vivid picture of the organization we want to be, without being overly constrained by the organization that we are today or were in the past. We strive to put into words what it would look like if we could bring the best of ideas and thoughts together and create a better future. Third, the visioning process builds cohesion. It brings together individuals from across the organization to focus on the long-term future. Beyond the output that it generates, the process is valuable because it enhances communication and understanding within the organization, and opens people's eyes to possibilities they may not have considered before. It creates a sense of shared ownership in the future, inspiring new initiatives. And it says, "We care," because we listen to each participant's input to evolve toward a shared vision.

Thoughtful participation from across the organization is crucial. People have to be well informed about the current state of the business. How can you talk about where you are going if you don't know where you're starting from? For this and other reasons, we operate with an unusual degree of transparency, providing far more information to people than is available in the vast majority of companies. Transparency ensures that people are aware of the current state of the business and also understand their role in ensuring its viability. As in sports, people need a scoreboard and a sense of where they are in the journey.

After every acquisition, we make a presentation about our culture and business success in order to engage our new team members. We also share with them information about the past performance of the business they were part of. Sharing such information builds trust and demonstrates integrity. At most of these presentations, people stare at us dumbfounded. They may have worked at the company for fifteen, twenty, twenty-five years and never seen any financial information. People are amazed that we trust them enough to share that information. Most private companies are fanatical about keeping financial information private. But can you imagine people playing a sport with passion if they don't know the score?

Creating a compelling vision and translating it into an actionable plan calls for a disciplined process. Visioning at most organizations takes months and involves multiple sessions with different groups. We have developed a focused visioning process that brings people together in a personally meaningful, deeply engaging, and often emotional experience to craft a great document within a couple of days. It works because it engages people, values all contributions, and creates a powerful group dynamic as the ideas are refined into a clear, concise, and compelling document.

Reflecting on our journey, we have found the following elements to be critical for cultural visioning:

1. **Purposeful Preparation.** A vision endures in part because of careful preparation and facilitation of the visioning session. While the final outcome is the reason people get

together, there's tremendous value in the process itself. We utilize pre-work in a meaningful way to bring people to an inspired place in advance, with insightful readings, videos, and reflective comments. This pre-work gives people the chance to hear the voices of their fellow attendees before they've even met, helps them hit the ground running, and creates strong unity in a short time.

2. **A Wide Variety of Participants.** The vision is not crafted by a team of senior leaders, but by a representative cross section of committed people with different perspectives invited to participate based on their leadership potential. They represent varied roles and businesses within the organization. We harness their collective wisdom and design the process so that everyone is heard and no one voice dominates.

3. **People Focus.** While most vision statements focus on products or services, our visions are about the impact we have on people's lives.

4. **Describe the Ideal State.** We focus not on who we think we are, but who we *want* to be. We encourage participants to think big, without fear of being pinned down to financial objectives or how we are going to achieve the vision. We engage in conversations about what is possible and paint a vivid picture of the ideal organization that we would want to create if we could remove all constraints.

Using Visioning to Solve Any Problem

At Barry-Wehmiller, we use visioning to address every significant challenge we face, including safety, team member wellness, and incentive alignment. The roots of this use of visioning go back to 1999.

We had just completed the acquisitions of Thiele, Accraply, Hayssen, and Bemis Packaging Machinery Company. For the first time, we had a group of divisional presidents connecting as peers and beginning to build relationships. Prior to these acquisitions, we had approached the market with a centralized sales organization to leverage the market presence and customer base of each of our companies. As we grew, we began to experience conflict in the marketplace that wasn't healthy for our sales team members or effective for customers. We had outgrown our approach to the market. The peer group of presidents tried to develop a better sales organization structure, but couldn't come to a consensus and asked for my help.

I had lost my voice that day, so I closed my office door to avoid having to talk and began to think about the problem. Rather than approaching the problem from the current state with all its organizational and relational challenges, I thought, "What should our ideal approach to the market look like?" I started to write down what I considered the "ideal behaviors of a sales executive."

When I was done, I invited a small, diverse group of team members to help me refine it. We came up with statements such as "We will operate from a foundation of trust. Shared information and open communication create competitive advantage. Participate when you can add value."

With a simple vision of how we wanted to behave in the marketplace, we asked ourselves, "What would cause people to behave that way?" Based on the responses we came up with, we reorganized the sales organization, implemented a new communication medium, put in place an incentive structure to encourage the right behavior, and developed recognition and celebration programs for those who embraced the change. Our focus was to create a more *efficient* approach to serve the market, to *enhance* the selling experience for our sales executives and for the customer, and to *empower* sales executives; therefore the program was called E^3.

Throughout the visioning process, Rhonda Spencer was preoccupied with the challenges that existed in the current state. I encouraged her to focus on what *could* be, not where we currently were. For example, when we designed the incentive program, she advocated putting in some safeguards to ensure that people followed the rules. I said, "No. We said we were going to trust people. Let's trust them to do the right thing, and we'll make changes if we need to." We trusted people, and they responded by acting in highly trustworthy ways.

In the first year of the program, we surfaced $20 million in opportunities that were shared across divisions, opportunities that we would not have seen without the E^3 program. The cultural environment changed virtually overnight.

Walking the Talk

Drafting a vision statement is relatively easy. What's critical is what you do with it once the document is written. It is essential to rapidly spread it throughout the organization and embed it deeply into people's heads and hearts. We do this through small-group sessions in which leaders communicate the vision and ask people to identify gaps between their experienced reality and the stated vision. When these gaps are identified, leaders take immediate steps to close them. If they cannot do so, they explain why.

A Vision for Safety

As a manufacturing company, safety is always at the forefront of our minds. Nobody gets out of bed in the morning and decides to come home without a finger or toe or suffer other serious injuries. Yet people often take excessive risks, despite the fine work of our safety committees and posters everywhere showing them how to stay safe.

In quick succession, we experienced some very serious accidents at a couple of our plants. In one case, a team member was about to machine a very large metal plate and didn't realize that the person who had worked on it before him hadn't clamped it down. It slid off and hit him on the foot, causing a crush injury that was so serious he lost half his foot. Another team member was working inside a large metal-bending machine. He asked his colleague who was working on the electrical panel, "Are you sure it's safe?"

The engineer replied, "Oh yeah, it's locked out." But it wasn't; the team member got pulled into the machine and was cut so badly that he almost bled to death.

These were terrible incidents, and we dealt with them the best we could. Soon after, one of our financial executives walked into our HR director's office and said, "We have a problem. Our worker's compensation costs are going up significantly. We have to do something or we're going to blow the budget."

As is our practice, we paused and stepped back to think about the issue in a deeper way. To connect it to our overall values and vision, we decided to do a visioning session on safety. We say, "We measure success by the way we touch the lives of people." What does that mean for safety? Is it really about worker's compensation costs and the number of lost days due to accidents? We didn't think so.

The team eventually came up with the following vision, which we call our Safety Covenant: "We commit to sending our team members home safely each day." In essence, we are simply saying, "We don't want our friends to get hurt."

We embraced this new vision of safety, and within a year, worker's compensation costs declined by half and have remained below industry averages. Why? Because we *inspired* safety instead of simply informing people about safe practices and inspecting for them. We did it from a place of caring more about people than about costs. We awakened people to our shared duty to look out for each other. Now all our people are vigilant about fixing anything, anywhere, that might be unsafe, that could possibly hurt them or one of their friends.

A good visioning process creates advocates for that way of being in the organization. People who participate in sessions are usually so energized by the experience that they become passionate ambassadors for the new vision. They start to live the vision and become visible symbols and ardent advocates for it within the organization.

John Quinn, president of Engle Martin (a Forsyth Capital portfolio company), talks about what it was like to have the participants return to the organization inspired by a new vision: "The cultural session to create 'The EM Way' was truly powerful, but the way we shared this vision throughout our organization in the weeks and months following the session was even more powerful. I created a video message to share with every associate in the organization. We then had senior staff speak with each of our regional offices in face-to-face dialogues. These dialogues were essential for two reasons. First, our professionals could see our body language and feel our commitment to this. Second, we could witness firsthand how they responded and address questions immediately with information and actions. We have embedded it into key organizational processes, including hiring, new employee orientation, and performance management. Over time, it has become anything but corporate wallpaper. It is something we all deeply believe in, and it has stood the test of time through the ups and downs of the market and multiple acquisitions."

There is an aliveness and vibrancy to all our vision statements. Our people don't view them as theoretical abstractions, and our leaders are regularly challenged to live up to them. People will say things like, "That's not very GPL." It is like a beacon from a lighthouse, ensuring that when we stray from the path—as we inevitably do at times—we can quickly correct our course.

We close with these reflections from Joe Wilhelm of the Design Group on what visioning has meant for the business and to him personally as a leader:

> *The original visioning exercise back in 2001 was initially somewhat unsettling. Setting a big, audacious goal is one thing, but no one wants to overcommit to the CEO of the company and then fall short. But over time, I came to appreciate that I had Bob's full confidence and support. It became apparent that the pursuit of highly ambitious growth goals was healthy for the organization, and that Bob did not intend to "penalize" us if we fell short of such goals. As we achieved a degree of success, it bred more and more confidence across the leadership team. Having an ambitious, principled vision empowered me to speak to the organization with a greater sense of our purpose. It encouraged the entire leadership team to think big,*

to "shoot for the stars." I personally began to think "outside the box"—in a responsible manner—without being constrained by conventional planning processes associated with budgetary goals.

Achieving greater success through the visioning process has enabled us to grow the team and advance the careers of our professionals at an accelerated pace. Growth led to promotions and career advancement within the organizational ranks. This part of the visioning process—what it means to people—has been the most gratifying for me. Ultimately, visioning has made me a much better leader. It is a core element of leadership in all organizations.

Chapter 8

| A New Way to Lead |

Steve Kreimer was a master assembler and expediter who became a supervisor in one of our BW Papersystems facilities. With his warm demeanor and southern drawl, Steve's personality gave him a softer touch than most traditional managers. He had worked in the Baltimore facility for more than twenty years before the company was acquired by Barry-Wehmiller.

Steve knew how to be a supervisor, having modeled his daily routine on his predecessor. He made sure people showed up on time, processed rework, expedited parts, and handled other issues as they came up. Steve always wanted to do the right thing; outside of work, he was a volunteer firefighter. He tried to be as people-centric as he could in a company with a traditional business mind-set. After the acquisition, we introduced our Guiding Principles of Leadership at the plant and suggested to him that he could be a leader, a steward of the new culture, a coach and mentor. He looked right back at us and said, "I would love to, but I have no idea what I'm supposed to do."

He continued, "I get the vision; in fact, I love the vision. But what exactly do you want me to *do* every day? I know exactly how to be a supervisor. But a leader? I have no idea how to be a leader. I don't know what leadership looks like."

Eighty percent of the people in most companies report to front-line leaders like Steve. Their way of leading *is* your culture. Steve's question was poignant and profound at the same time. He was inspired and eager to accept the awesome responsibility of leadership. But that can't be translated into action unless we are able to teach people not only the technical skills of their role, but also what it *means* to be a leader.

The Idea of a Leadership Checklist

When pilots prepare for flight, they must perform a rigorous safety review of the aircraft, guided by a detailed checklist—not once a month or even once a day, but each and every time they fly. Pilots and their passengers are not the only people who benefit from a checklist. In the United States, an estimated 440,000 people die annually because of medical errors in hospitals.[1] Hospital-acquired infections are almost entirely preventable. In 2001, Peter Pronovost, an intensive-care specialist physician at Johns Hopkins Hospital in Baltimore, Maryland, came up with a simple, five-item checklist to remind physicians to take basic safety measures. The result: At test sites in Michigan, hospital-acquired infections dropped from 2.7 per 1,000 patients to virtually zero in three months. Over 1,500 lives were saved in the first eighteen months, saving the state of Michigan $100 million. It is estimated that Dr. Pronovost's simple idea has saved more lives than the work of any laboratory scientist over the last decade.[2] In addition, huge numbers of people have been spared needless suffering and prolonged hospital stays. Of course, it seems like just common sense, but the reality is that "common sense is rarely common practice." Even today, many doctors and hospitals ignore this simple practice.

With these two templates, we were inspired to create a "leadership checklist" that describes the essential actions that leaders within our organization must take every day. It is not much of a leap to say that leaders too have precious lives in their care every day, just as pilots and physicians do. How those people are treated during the course of the workday determines how they are when they reach home—surly and drained or happy and fulfilled. We set out to translate the Guiding Principles of Leadership document from a vision statement hanging on a wall into a working document that people could carry in their pockets and live by every day.

We began by asking leaders throughout our organization, "What does a Barry-Wehmiller leader Be, Know, and Do?" These are the three dimensions of the US Army's leadership model. "Be" is about your character as a leader, who you are as a person. It is about being aware of your personal values and being aligned with the organization's values, which for the Army are loyalty, duty, respect, selfless service, honor, integrity, and personal courage. "Know" is about the knowledge and skills necessary to be a good leader. For the Army, these are interpersonal, conceptual, technical, and tactical skills. "Do" is about actions—the behaviors that leaders engage in. They include influencing, operating, and improving.[3]

Leadership Checklist

I accept the awesome responsibility of leadership. The following statements describe my essential actions as a leader.

◇ I practice stewardship of the Guiding Principles of Leadership through my time, conversations, and personal development.
◇ I advocate safety and wellness through my actions and words.

- ◇ I reflect to lead my team in Achieving Principled Results on Purpose.
- ◇ I inspire passion, optimism, and purpose.
- ◇ My personal communication cultivates fulfilling relationships.
- ◇ I foster a team community in which we are committed to each other and to the pursuit of a common goal.
- ◇ I exercise responsible freedom, empowering each of us to achieve our potential.
- ◇ I proactively engage in the personal growth of individuals on my team.
- ◇ I facilitate meaningful group interactions.
- ◇ I set, coach to, and measure goals that define winning.
- ◇ I recognize and celebrate the greatness in others.
- ◇ I commit to daily continuous improvement.

When we engage our heads, hearts, and hands around these habits, extraordinary levels of trust and fulfillment will result.

Once we had generated a list of qualities, competencies, and behaviors through this process, we made sure they were in harmony with the Guiding Principles of Leadership. Using our visioning process, and input from our leaders on more than 250 different traits and characteristics, we created our Leadership Checklist—leadership behaviors that we could train to in our organization that would impact the daily life of the people in the business.

At Barry-Wehmiller, we refer frequently to "the awesome responsibility of leadership." This is an acknowledgment that being a leader means actively choosing to be a good steward of the lives entrusted to you. You may have a leadership title, but that doesn't necessarily mean you've accepted the true responsibility of leadership. When we teach leadership, we encourage participants to think deeply about the choice they are making and to consider leadership as a conscious commitment rather than a title or a role description.

Accepting the awesome responsibility of leadership at Barry-Wehmiller means internalizing and focusing on every item in the Leadership Checklist every day. It means continuously educating and developing yourself to become a better leader. We ask people to unlearn much of what they have already learned, critically examine their past practices, and determine what they can do differently to live our truly human leadership model. Our Leadership Fundamentals course includes an in-depth focus on each of the twelve items in the Leadership Checklist.

An important take-away for participants learning our approach to leadership is that they can be—indeed, must be—the same person at work that they are at home. They don't need to wear a mask to work. The Leadership Checklist is not just for the eight or ten hours people spend in the office or in the factory. It's for all twenty-four hours and every aspect of their life.

Reflecting this, the comments people make after taking Leadership Fundamentals have more to do with their marriage, parenting, and relationships with family members than with work. Of course, we do see tremendous performance benefits and personal growth at work. Each one of us is, after all, one person, though we wear different hats at home and at work. We naturally bring skills and perspectives that we develop at work back into the home, and we bring things we develop at home to our workplace. These skills impact our most important relationships at home and work.

Carol O'Neill is our VP of strategy, technology, and key initiatives.

She finds great value in the Leadership Checklist as a way to develop good leadership habits:

> When I first saw the checklist, I thought that in some ways it is really obvious: It was a list of things that you should do as a leader. For me personally, even though I think I am wired to be a good person, I am not really that good about recognition. Unfortunately, I end up dwelling on what didn't work so well instead of on what did. I decided to turn the leadership checklist into a spreadsheet, with "Weeks" written across the top. At the end of each week, I ask myself, "In the course of the week, did I practice these things as a leader? What did I do to proactively create an environment where everybody goes home in one piece, with as many fingers and toes as they came to work with?" If, at the end of the week, I couldn't say what I had done to advance that in a proactive way, I would ask myself, "What should I have done based on the experiences I had this week, and what should I make a point of doing next week?" I think it's really important to keep track of that.

Jay Deitz, manufacturing director at BW Papersystems, was part of the team that developed the Leadership Checklist. He remembers feeling strongly about including "inspiration" as a key element in the checklist:

> We were brainstorming as a group on the Leadership Checklist. Once we had all the ideas up, we categorized them using the affinity process. We had about ten categories on the board. I found that "inspiration" was missing from the list. At that time, I was a front-line leader in the organization. Despite some trepidation, I decided to lobby the group to include inspiration.

In my life experiences, I had found nothing to be more important than inspiration. I coached at the national and international level in cross-country skiing. My daughter was the national champion, and so I had the privilege of working with elite athletes and recognizing how far people could go if they were inspired. Experts tell us that athletes are not capable of exceeding certain performance levels. Throughout my life, I have seen that once emotion kicks in and you have passion, potential just opens up. Because of this, I felt very strongly about getting inspiration into our checklist.

It took some convincing to get the team to accept the idea, but they eventually did. Soon after, Bob Chapman came to meet with our team for a report on our work. After reviewing the twelve leadership points we had included, Bob's response was to say that "inspiration" was one of the most important points, if not the most important.

My personal inspiration comes from serving our people and living up to our principles. I have two things framed on the wall in my office. Behind me is a poster-size picture of our entire staff. So I continually have my team looking over my shoulder! To my right, I have a large poster with the Guiding Principles of Leadership. Every single day, when people come to my office and we are talking about decisions we're going to make or challenges that we face, I can refer either to the picture behind me or to the Guiding Principles of Leadership to my right.

———

We have found three master keys to our leadership culture—deep listening, authentic vulnerability, and courageous patience.

Listening is a greatly undervalued skill in our organizations and in our culture. The conventional wisdom is that leaders tell people what to do and how to act. We have found that the most powerful thing a leader can do is to truly and deeply listen. This is at the core of our powerful Communication Skills Training class, which is a prerequisite for several courses within Barry-Wehmiller University. As leadership expert Kevin Cashman says, "How often do we pause to be genuinely present with someone? How often do we really hear what the other person is saying and feeling versus filtering it heavily through our own immediate concerns and time pressures? Authentic listening is not easy. We hear the words, but rarely do we really slow down to listen and squint with our ears to hear the emotions, fears, and underlying concerns. . . . Not only will this help you to understand the value and contribution the other person brings, it will create a new openness in the relationship that will allow you to express yourself and be heard more authentically as well."[4]

Vulnerability is also key. We teach our leaders to share their strengths as well as their challenges. This creates an environment where others feel comfortable to share. We half-jokingly say that our learning experiences are measured in "man tears." It is not easy for people to overcome years of conditioning and allow themselves to be vulnerable in front of their colleagues. But it is not possible to create a truly open and caring culture if people consistently put on a mask and armor when they go to work.

The third quality is courageous patience. This is so unusual in today's business world that it is worth exploring in some detail.

Courageous Patience

Our philosophy of "courageous patience" has been a key factor in our transformation. Culture is a huge flywheel: If you're willing to be patient and stay true to the vision, you'll eventually see results both culturally and financially. But it takes time to build up momentum and get up to speed. Patience requires the ability to see beyond the immediate to the greater opportunity that our vision promises. We focus on what is working and are incredibly patient with those who don't seem to "get it."

You *must* be patient with people, because you don't know what they have been through. In his book *See You at the Top*, Zig Ziglar illustrates this with a parable. If you put some fleas inside a jar and close the lid, they immediately start jumping and trying to escape. After hitting the lid repeatedly, the fleas eventually realize that they cannot escape and stop trying. They still jump, just not as high. If you now remove the lid, the fleas keep jumping, but not high enough to escape the jar. They don't even notice that the lid is no longer in place.

You see this all the time in organizations. People are products of their experiences. We don't know what kinds of "lids" they've experienced. Even if someone else put the lid on the jar, it's our job as leaders to remove the lid and let people know that it is safe to jump high again.

We encourage people to think about patience in terms of years, rather than months. There are people in our acquired companies who are so broken and carry so much baggage from past experiences that it can take us years to overcome their cynicism and restore trust. It's worth the wait, because such individuals often become the most passionate and effective exemplars and advocates for our culture. They then say to us, "Be patient with this next person—I can relate to where they are, because that is exactly where I was." These former cynics become outstanding facilitators in our process-improvement journey, celebrated professors in our university, senior leaders in our businesses, and sources of inspiration to everyone.

Bill Ury uses a vivid metaphor to describe our philosophy of courageous patience: "It's like you are driving a bus around the block repeatedly. You keep picking people up when they are ready, when they choose to opt in. But you stick to your values and your direction and patiently wait for people to hop on board." People know that the bus will come around again, and there will be room on it for everyone, and no one will blame them for not getting on sooner. To extend the metaphor, it is a safe business (a stable business), and the driver (leader) knows the destination (vision) and the best route to get there (process and culture).

Rhonda Spencer recalls an experience at BW Papersystems in the northern Wisconsin woods:

> As we began to try to bring about the culture envisioned in our GPL document, we tried a number of different things. At the Phillips, Wisconsin, location, we had a focus group session to talk about how we were doing in living this culture. Well, that opened up a can of worms! It put our small group in the tough position of having to hear a lot of complaints and concerns about the gaps between our vision and reality. I committed to go up to Phillips to listen to these team members and help them understand where we were on the journey. After I sat and listened and talked to the group for a few hours, they said, "You should be having this conversation with every person in the Phillips organization."
>
> I said, "OK, I will." (This is an interesting lesson in communi-

cation. We always think we're doing a great job communicating, but in fact we can never communicate enough.) So I had series of conversations (now known as the "cabin sessions") at the Marschke Cabin in Phillips with all 400 team members, twenty at a time.

In one of the sessions I was talking about trust, and a woman from the back of the room yelled, "I don't trust you at all, lady!"

I thought for a minute and said, "Well, I don't blame you. You've been through a lot here, and I imagine it's hard to believe that the things we're telling you are true and that we're sincere. I guess we need to earn your trust." That was such an interesting revelation for me personally; having grown up at Barry-Wehmiller and having had the benefit of being led by so many leaders who always had my best interest at heart, I developed a new level of empathy for what people in the companies we've acquired had been through.

The story of Randall Fleming, a welder in the fabrication department at BW Papersystems, exemplifies our commitment to courageous patience. Randall, who used to be known as Randy, is a former member of the US military. He stands about six foot two and has been a body-builder all his life. Randy was a self-described storm trooper in the back of our facility; most people did not want to go anywhere near his part of the shop, and he liked it that way. Outside of work, he played in a heavy-metal rock band and wore a black cowboy hat, sunglasses, and a long trench coat. He looked like a demon out of hell staring out at the crowd. That was the mind-set he brought to Barry-Wehmiller. It was shaped by experiences in his personal life and at work, which had seemingly drained the humanity out of him.

In 2006, our process-improvement journey was being launched in Phillips. Randy's response was, "I want nothing to do with this. This is

just a corporate ploy to get us to work harder and get more out of us."
He said this loudly and repeatedly, and actively discouraged people
from participating in improvement events.

Here is Randall in his own words describing his journey:

*I came here from the military, and didn't have any schooling as
far as a trade of any type. I was working my way up to become a
fabricator, and it was a very aggressive work environment. We had
four supervisors who circled throughout the work areas all day,
making sure everyone was working. There was very little information sharing because they didn't feel that we needed to know much.
I had no idea who the senior leaders were. We did not have a very
good relationship with our engineering staff, mainly because we
blamed each other for all the problems we had. It was old-school
manufacturing: You came to work every day, didn't ask any questions or make any waves, and made sure that you got your work
done.*

*That was my first ten or fifteen years in the manufacturing world.
When Barry-Wehmiller acquired us, big changes happened. They
brought in the idea of Lean manufacturing, which was a whole new
concept to us. They also started to go in the direction of what they call
a "people-centric culture." To a guy who was brought up through the
military and then in a manufacturing environment where you don't
ask questions, just do your job, this was a very foreign concept. Not
only did I not believe it, but I fought against it, because it was so
different from how I was raised. I can tell you now that it's one of the
most open environments I've ever experienced, 180 degrees different
from how it was before.*

The turning point for me was four years ago, when I decided to leave the company because I wanted to do more with my life. I had evolved quite a bit personally, realized that I wanted to be more of a help to people, but couldn't find a way to do it. When I talked to one of our senior leaders, Jay Deitz, about quitting, he offered me opportunities to stay here and make a difference. It was unbelievable to me; somebody actually said, "We're going to give you an opportunity to do what you want to do."

A good friend of mine—my chiropractor, Tim Wakefield—had heard Bob Chapman speak, and said to me, "Why don't you try taking one of these courses? If you don't see any value, I'll help you move."

Well, I stayed, and am I ever glad I did! I am now a professor in Barry-Wehmiller University. I teach the Inspiration module for our Leadership Fundamentals course, and I also teach Inspiring Responsible Change. I went from the guy who didn't want to do it to now teaching it!

Everything about me is different, and everything in my life has changed. I see my daughters, Alicia and Jenna, every couple of months, and every time I'm with them they tell me that I've changed some more. They can't believe the type of person I'm becoming. It makes me happy, and it also makes me sad, because I wish I could have been that all along for them. They are my best friends now. My parents and I have a much better relationship than we ever had. I don't have the same friends anymore, I have different friends who are more like me now: they want to have an impact in the world and on the people around them. It's opened my eyes to the possibility that even though I'm fifty-two years old, I can still make a difference in the world. I'm more excited about where I'm at in my life now than I've ever been.

Randy is now a leader in our continuous-improvement journey, meaning he is a master facilitator of kaizen events and other improvement projects. (*Kaizen* is a Japanese word made up of two distinct characters: *kai*, meaning "change," and *zen*, meaning "good." So "kaizen" simply means "change for the good.") He is probably the most vocal champion of our continuous-improvement journey throughout all of Phillips. As a professor of inspiration in our Leadership Fundamentals course, he teaches other people how to tap into their own personal inspiration and how to inspire others. The storm trooper who stood in the back of the facility yelling, "Don't trust them!" is now one of the greatest advocates for inspiration and improvement in our entire organization. He has touched numerous lives across the organization—almost every one of the 630+ lives at BW Papersystems in Phillips, in addition to many others throughout North America. He now teaches and speaks to people from our European operations as well. He's interacted with senior leaders, high-level customers, local business leaders, and others who are interested in learning about our culture. People have urged him to write a book about his journey of transformation and growth, of moving from isolation and hostility to openness and caring. Randy is a man reborn, and it is incredibly inspiring to see. In fact, he has changed so much that he no longer uses the name Randy and prefers to be called Randall.

If we had given Randall only three or six months, if we hadn't shown courageous patience, he never would have had his personal transformation, and he would've never become an exemplary leader, a shining light for our entire organization. It has been immensely personally rewarding for Randall and others like him, and it has had enduring benefits for our culture. People see that we were willing to have patience with Randall, that there were no hard feelings, and that he's now held up across the organization. Randy morphing into Randall has inspired many others to go through their own transformations as well.

The People Are Fine

One great truth that we've learned is this: *The people are just fine; it's our leadership that's lacking*. When people perform poorly, most leaders are quick to blame them, perhaps even fire them right away. It takes introspection and humility to admit, "That might be a consequence of my poor leadership." This is what separates Jay Deitz from ordinary leaders. Rather than sitting on the sidelines during the creation of the Leadership Checklist or assuming that Randy was a bad apple who needed to move on, Jay was willing to accept the awesome responsibility of leadership. Without leaders like Jay in the organization, the Randys would have moved on or been pushed out long ago.

Let's continue our story about Steve Kreimer, one of our supervisors in Baltimore, Maryland. Steve, like Jay, was one of the first people who strongly resonated with our Guiding Principles of Leadership and the Leadership Checklist. He made them daily aspects of what he did as a leader in our manufacturing and assembly areas. Steve changed his part of the organization from a traditional silo structure to a "value stream" organization that put everyone in his group on one team, striving to better meet the needs of the organization and of customers. He started to hold people up as shining lights, celebrating the great things they were doing. His success at work cascaded into his personal life and his life as a volunteer firefighter. Based on the skills he had developed at Barry-Wehmiller, he led the largest fund-raiser for his fire station in its history, securing enough funding to build an entirely new station. Eventually, he was selected as the chief of that station. While we were sad to see him leave our organization, we were happy that we had the opportunity to share in his journey for a period of time. He is still part of our family, a valued alumnus who is continuing to help us advance our larger purpose of enabling greater joy and fulfillment through the way we lead and work.

Jay Deitz is still amazed at the Barry-Wehmiller approach to people:

> *The environment prior to Barry-Wehmiller buying us was as fractured as you can get. After Barry-Wehmiller acquired us, I saw the culture go from one extreme to the other. One important point, and this really speaks to Bob's brand of leadership, is that we didn't change any of the team members after the acquisition. Barry-Wehmiller was relatively new to this when they acquired us; at the time, we were their largest acquisition. I have been able to participate in many acquisitions since then. We have learned a lot about how to acquire companies. But something that hasn't changed is that when Barry-Wehmiller comes in, we don't change the employees, as in replacing them; we do change them in a huge way over time in terms of their attitude, engagement, and fulfillment. Typically, management says that the employees are the problem. Barry-Wehmiller acquires companies that face severe challenges and aren't viewed as having much potential and brings to them a unique blend of strategy and culture that allows them to create a much better future.*

We will close this chapter with this from Randall Fleming:

> *The message that I would love to see carried into the world is the message that I think all of us at Barry-Wehmiller who are on this journey want to see: that there is still hope—not only for manufac-*

turing in the United States because of the manufacturing renaissance that we are a part of—but for people all around this world. We can truly build a better world if we embrace what we're trying to do in the manufacturing culture of Barry-Wehmiller; we can change the world for the better, one person at a time. We can wake up every day to a brighter future. We can do this by doing what we teach here at Barry-Wehmiller, which is "Live from your values and do what's right." That includes caring for each other. I never used to care about anyone other than my family, and now I care about everyone. If we all get up every day and do what's right, how can anything be bad?

Chapter 9

| Humanizing the Process |

In the plush conference room, it was all smiles and handshakes between the Barry-Wehmiller sales team and the potential customer dangling a $5 million sale before them. Dressed in their wing-tipped shoes and fancy suits, the salesmen collectively held their breath as they came to the final and most critical aspect of the visit: the plant tour. "Let's just show the machine performance and get the hell out," was the general sentiment. "Let's pray they don't notice anything else going on out there."

But even before the double doors to the factory swung shut behind the group, it was too late. One of the customers pointed to the back corner on the left and whispered something to his colleague with a smirk. It was clear that they had spotted him: Jimmy Hughes, thirty-year veteran machinist in our BW Papersystems division in Baltimore. He was napping against his machine again, head burrowed in his forearm, eyes closed. One salesman shook his head. "Lazy good-for-nothing. He just doesn't give a damn! Why do we keep this guy around?" he thought, as he hurried the customer group along, embarrassed for what was going on in the plant.

Fast-forward ten years. Jimmy Hughes is the number-one stop on every customer tour in the facility, and people often trail behind the group to ask him extra questions. He now leads a team of six people and has never been more fulfilled, animated, or optimistic. "What happened?" you might ask. We will get to that. But first, here is Jimmy describing what his life used to be like:

> *I consider myself a blue-collar worker. I don't use big words like "empowerment" and "fulfillment" like the big shots in the office. But I have always tried to do an honest day's work for an honest day's pay.*
>
> *Misunderstood. That was me for most of my career. A lot of suits kept changing in the head office, using a lot of flowery words about culture. But they never understood much about what I do. I work with my hands, I get dirty and I am proud of it—because I take a raw piece of steel and transform it into something useful, something that helps make the boxes that almost everything comes packaged in. I bet you know people like me—chugging away at a job, trying to support a family, carrying a few extra pounds around the middle and too few hairs on my head, taking chaos and making something valuable out of it. But through it all, always misunderstood and unappreciated.*
>
> *Ten years ago, if you came by my area, here is what you would see. A man with his full weight leaned up against the side of a machine, eyes closed, trying to grab a few minutes of peace. It looked like I was taking a nap, and sometimes it ended up that way. Lazy. Troublemaker. That is what people saw me as. More than once, I know they asked themselves if they needed to keep someone like me around.*
>
> *No one ever came closer or stayed long enough to understand. My machine runs thirty to forty-five minutes at a time. I was told that I had to stay close by to make sure nothing went wrong. It's boring as hell—like watching the washing machine run. But I was*

all alone in the back corner of this dark, greasy shop. I couldn't leave to get material for the next job while the machine was running, and I couldn't control what came into my station or where items went when I was done. That didn't stop the complaining. Nearly every hour, someone with a title would come by and yell, asking why their part wasn't done yet. So I would stop what I was doing and work on their part. The next hour someone else with a fancy title would come by and tell me to stop what I was doing and work on their part.

Do you want to know the worst of it? On the way to the lunch-room every day, I walked past the inventory rack where my parts eventually wound up. Those parts that were so important to the big shots? They would still be sitting there a week later, gathering dust. Nothing to show for getting chewed out and keeping my machine running for eight long hours each day.

The Power of Process

Think about all the Jimmys in your organization and what they are up against. Do you know a friend or family member who feels this way? In most organizations today, there are far too many Jimmys battling and being worn down by archaic systems and indifferent leadership.

In all those years, no one gave Jimmy the opportunity to do things differently. There was nothing for him to do while his machine was running except to slump up against it and look like he was taking a nap. He hadn't designed his work flow that way; the previous leaders of the business had. Here was a great opportunity for a caring leader to find a new way to lead Jimmy, to allow him to take responsibility for his area and redesign the work that he was part of. We just had to figure out how to make that happen.

In another part of the same factory in Baltimore, we launched a journey of continuous improvement, using the tools of Lean, with the courage to ask our associates what could be better. The first response was silence. People were hesitant to speak up, wondering if this was the latest cost-cutting ploy or more hot air from senior leaders. Many skipped the meeting at which the new program was announced, confident it would fizzle out in a few months.

It took humility for senior leaders to stand up in front of a roomful of veteran team members and say, "All these years, we had it wrong. Help us make it right. Show us how." This was the start of the first continuous-improvement event: ten people working together for five days to make things better. There were no ranks, titles, or degrees in the room. On the fourth day, many in the team were still skeptical—until one of the six-ton machine tools that had been rooted to its spot for decades was slowly lifted off its footing and relocated to where the team had suggested. You could almost hear people's minds changing in that instant—maybe this new way of doing things was real, after all!

Whether it's manufacturing, education, or health care, we can all relate to the six-ton sacred cows in our environment, old ways of doing business that everyone knows are out of place but that seem too big to move. They stand like huge multistory buildings blocking the path to humanity in our processes.

The second five-day improvement event was in Jimmy's area, and it wasn't until the third day that he said more than three words. But something happened on that third day that pushed Jimmy over the edge. He recalls:

During that first event, I just wanted to keep my head down, but finally by the third day, I figured it couldn't get much worse, so why not share an idea? I wouldn't have believed it, but they took my idea and put it at the top of the list—so I kept sharing. I told them a lot over the next two days and the following weeks and months: how we could schedule better, how I could do things while the machine ran, how we could run faster.

Today I still wear a blue collar to work, and I still get dirty turning steel into something of value. But I lead six people who run the twelve machines in our part of the factory. We schedule our own work, we decide when to purchase more material, and we see the product of our labor put on a machine within days, sometimes hours after we get it done.

So many people want to know how we do it. We have a tour come through here almost every other day. Two years ago, we had an astronaut come to learn from us. Last year, the governor of Maryland came by and shook my hand because now I am the number-one tour stop. I am not always sure why they want to listen to me, but they do.

I don't have too many more years left here, but my son now works in the business. He took the Lean class and now leads our maintenance group's efforts to make work better for everyone. And guess what, the new Lean leader cut his teeth as a night-shift machinist with me twenty years ago. When he gets stuck, he still comes to me for help.

"We Don't Pay You to Think"

Larry Pierquet, a mandrel assembler in our PCMC organization in Green Bay, was with us for forty-five years and became affectionately known as the poster child for our continuous-improvement effort. He experienced one of our first improvement events. Before it started, he wondered, "What are we going to talk about for five whole days? I've been making these parts for years. They're not complex, and we know how to make them. What could be the focus of all this time together?" He told us that he didn't even want to participate because of something that happened to him forty-two years before: As a young machinist, he was having trouble creating a part and went to his supervisor holding the mangled part. He started to say, "I think that if we just change this . . . ," but the supervisor interrupted him: "Stop right there. We don't pay you to think. Go back to your machine and make the part right this time."

From that moment on, Larry didn't share any more ideas for improvement with the organization. He maintained his silence for forty-two years! Through the course of the continuous -improvement event, Larry finally opened up and shared some of his ideas. He saw that they were taken seriously and implemented right away. He stood up at the end of the event and said that he would be "an ambassador of this program because everybody was treated with respect and dignity, something that's too often lost in our organization." A few months later, his words rang through the halls of the Lean Enterprise Institute's international conference. After all those decades of silence, Larry became an effusive ambassador for our approach to Lean.

Another machinist in our PCMC organization named Chris Charniak said, "You know, sometimes when I run my machines I just feel like a robot. All I do during the day is push a button and turn something on, then it happens and I take the part out and I push the button again. It's not very fulfilling." Chris is still a machinist in our organization, but he has also stepped up to be a Lean event facilitator. Instead of continuing to function as a robot, he focused on maximizing the impact of his machine in his area and then began to teach others how to do that. He has touched the entire organization with his ability to help others make their workplaces more effective.

———

We can bring humanity and dignity back to the workplace by inviting people to own the process. Machines, systems, and procedures exist to serve people, not the other way around. Through the right approach to continuous improvement, we can find the humility, courage, and creativity to put things in their proper place and restore the primacy of people over all else.

Where did we lose our way with business processes? When did we start using them to shackle instead of serve people? It goes back to the industrial revolution, which was all about leveraging mass production processes; people came off the farms, where they had agricultural crafts, and many lost the dignity of work. Recall Alexis de Tocqueville's shock when he visited factories in Manchester, England, in 1835: "Here humanity attains its most complete development and its most brutish; here civilization works its miracles, and civilized man is turned back almost into a savage."[1]

Used properly, Lean offers a unique opportunity to free people to truly contribute their gifts and talents, to see and participate in different parts of the process, to rise above being robots, to contribute in new ways and always be thinking about how to make things better. Unfortunately, a large majority of companies that begin the journey ultimately fail to become truly Lean. Let's unpack that for just a moment. Why would anyone consider starting a journey with a 3 percent success rate?[2]

First of all, virtually all organizations embrace Lean solely to improve quality and profitability. Second, people see the tools but miss the larger opportunity to listen to the people who know how to do it better. Waste elimination alone isn't inspiring; inspiration comes when people like Jimmy and Larry are truly listened to and engaged in the process. Finally, people lack patience and commitment; a journey like this doesn't end in six months or a year, but lasts a lifetime.

Lean with Compassion

Lean is a disciplined process of continuous improvement traditionally focused on minimizing waste and maximizing customer value. The nonprofit Lean Enterprise Institute states: "Lean means creating more value for customers with fewer resources. A Lean organization understands customer value and focuses its key processes to continuously increase it. The ultimate goal is to provide perfect value to the customer through a perfect value creation process that has zero waste."[3] As you can see, *people*—the ones actually creating the value—are nowhere to be found in that description.

The foundation of Lean is the 5S tool from the Toyota Production System. It is based on five Japanese words: *seiri, seiton, seiso, seiketsu,* and *shitsuke,* which can be roughly translated as "sort," "straighten," "shine," "standardize," and "sustain."[4] 5S is a systemic visual management tool focused on eliminating waste in processes to drive greater efficiency; its goal is to make problems easy to spot and correct.

At Barry-Wehmiller, we have expanded 5S to 7S, adding "safety" and "satisfaction" to better align with our people-centered vision. We start with the idea of keeping our friends safe, so safety is our first S, and no event is complete without ensuring that we've achieved satisfaction for the people who work in the affected area.

7S is our foundation for Lean because it achieves several essential things:

◇ Helps people look at their workplace through the lens of continuous improvement.

◇ Allows people to see tangible changes in the workplace in a few short days.

◇ Empowers individuals to look at their workspace and self-select items to eliminate; you must clear out the clutter before you have room to add in new behaviors.

◇ Breaks down silos: All 7S events have cross-functional teams. This is where engineers who have been designing parts for twenty years and machinists who have been building parts for twenty years meet, often for the first time.

◇ Establishes a rhythm and discipline to improving, checking, and improving some more.

Lean ideas are typically deployed in kaizen events. As explained earlier, the word *kaizen* means "change for the good." Traditional Lean practitioners usually define *good* as measurable business improvements. To us, it prioritizes the good of the individual actually doing the work, making the work easier and less frustrating.

When we began this journey, we sat down with our associates, shared our vision, as we had done with the Guiding Principles of Leadership, and listened. Many people had experienced traditional Lean implementations at other companies, and more than a few had family members or friends let go from a company that had gone "lean and mean." They were understandably cynical. We worked to convince them that our approach would be different. The differences are summarized in the table below.

Category	Traditional Lean	Barry-Wehmiller	Why
What is it called?	Lean	L³—Living Legacy of Leadership	What you call something matters. L³ is a way of leading and a more human way of living, not a cost-reduction process.
What is the focus in finding areas of improvement?	Waste	Frustration	Waste is about things; focusing on frustration makes it human.
How do we engage people for continuous improvement?	Mandating	Listening	Some traditional Lean leaders come in like dictators, saying, "This is how we are going to do things," and they start requiring people to attend training classes. We try to create "pull" for change in our people. That starts with listening with vulnerability and helping people let go of baggage.
How do we think about process?	Process vs. People	People and Process	Some Lean leaders see the process focus as a way to drive out human error and human engagement; our approach is about bringing greater humanity to the process. The process must serve the people, not the other way around.

Realizing the Vision Through Continuous Improvement

Our continuous-improvement journey has been essential to the success of so many things that we believe. Vision is essential and is the first step. But it's one thing to have a vision of an ideal future state; without a way to engage people in creating that ideal future, it remains just words on the wall. Lean gives us the tools to engage our team members in creating the future we've collectively envisioned. We changed the name from Lean to L^3 (Living Legacy of Leadership) because in the early stages of embracing these powerful leadership ideas, it became clear to us that Lean as widely practiced was mostly about numbers and not about people. If the Toyota production processes had been studied and named properly, it would have been called Listen. We believed it could be the most powerful process for continuous improvement if it was thoughtfully aligned with truly human leadership.

An example is our process for managing cash. Cash is the lifeblood of any business, and we have a disciplined process for managing it. This grew out of our challenging experiences in the '80s and '90s. Over time, there was a sense that our cash management policies were not in alignment with our vision to positively touch the lives of people who are responsible for and impacted by these practices. When this challenge was raised, we decided to have a kaizen event to address it. The focus was to define a process that would maintain the critical disciplines for the financial security of the company, empower our team members on the front line of supplier relationships with greater autonomy in the disbursement of payments, and align our behavior to our vision to positively touch the lives of our vendors.

Naturally, a vision creates a gap between where we are today and where we desire to be. Lean is the combination of mind-sets, tools, and facilitated interactions that help us:

◇ Define where we are currently (you can't describe the gap if you don't know where you are).

◇ Consider the gap from multiple perspectives (cross-functional, not just silo-based thinking).

◇ Engage people in the process (people are much more invested if they are part of defining and closing the gap).

◇ Brainstorm creative countermeasures to close the gap.

◇ Implement, observe, test, and refine countermeasures.

◇ Recognize and celebrate accomplishments at defined milestones.

Leaders who don't appreciate Lean make the error of casting great visions and getting people excited but then falling back into command-and-control management. Lean traditionalists make the error of implementing Lean without a compelling vision, so that improvements are made but ultimately undermine the culture rather than galvanizing it.

Jay Deitz recalls the impact that L^3 had after years of struggle to implement traditional Lean thinking: "The L^3 vision uniquely blends the personal touch, making the individual important, and Lean. That's what has enabled us to succeed. There were a number of things about Lean that were very difficult for us. Lean came out of the context of repetitive manufacturing—car builders, widget makers, things like that. We're not a widget factory. We build high-variability, low-volume equipment. We don't repeat our processes very often. So there wasn't a magic silver bullet for Lean in our organization, and we couldn't see anybody who had it. We recognized pretty quickly that the coupling of the people-centric mind-set with Lean created this unique combination that enabled us to experience new growth and fulfillment. When the ingredients came together, we started to see results. We continue to improve it, but it's a unique recipe that nobody else had a handle on when we started on this journey."

At the conclusion of every L³ event or project, participants host a report-out session to share their improvements with other members of the organization. Traditionally, this ends with the final numbers—how much time or space or money was saved—and everyone applauds and thanks the team.

One day, in the same Baltimore plant that Jimmy calls home, I sat in on such a session. After the team finished sharing their improvement numbers—which were dramatic enough to be excited about—I asked from the back of the room, "How did it make you feel?"

The leader of the event was a little taken aback. After a moment of reflection, he said, "If I knew earlier what I know now about how to interact with people and solve problems, my marriage wouldn't have ended in divorce."

Dick Ryan, our Lean journey leader, has spent decades in the field of Lean and is a strong advocate. He said his "aha" moment was when we asked people that question. Grown men cry in trying to respond. Now, in a practice that is unique to Barry-Wehmiller, we make sure that every report-out session is about more than numerical outcomes; we always make it a point to ask, "How does this make you feel?" The responses are priceless, genuine reflections of the impact our L³ journey has on people's lives. We capture the most compelling comments on film and share them throughout the organization.

We have now completed over 500 continuous-improvement events with over 3,000 participants. Dick Ryan says, "At the outset of our Lean journey, we realized that to build a great manufacturing company, keep jobs in local communities, and positively touch people's lives, we needed to change. As we combine these leadership practices with Lean tools, Barry-Wehmiller is taking Lean to another level." Dennis Butz, value stream manufacturing leader at PCMC, says, "It's amazing to see how far we have come on our journey in such a short period. Who would have thought that asking people, 'What do you think?' would have brought us so far?"

Process Parables

The accounts payable office in one of our divisions was a disorganized mess. Work piled up hourly, without an end in sight. People would pick up the top invoice from a stack, work on it for as long as necessary, and then pull the next one. At the end of the day, the stack could be as high as or even higher than when they walked in, giving the team no sense of progress or winning. It was dispiriting and dehumanizing, with people robotically doing the same thing day after day. They had no opportunity or inspiration to use their head and heart to make things better.

We launched a Lean initiative there and invited people to own the process. We helped them develop a vision, put them in the structured environment of a kaizen event, and asked, "How can we change this process?"

First, we divided the invoices into buckets, reordering the work so that people would have a sense of accomplishment when they finished the last invoice for the day. They could also look at the next day's work and the days after that to get a sense of the work to come. Second, we separated the more complex invoices from the straightforward ones. A simple invoice only takes five minutes to put through; the complex ones could take more than half an hour and require five phone calls to resolve. People could feel a sense of accomplishment and movement by getting through as many simple invoices as possible. They could then collaborate with other team members in a daily meeting called the Hospital Bed Meeting (to treat the sickest patients, in this case the most complex invoices) and quickly get the answers they needed. They didn't need to make any calls, because everybody was already in the room. Together, we had taken a broken process, made it very freeing, and filled it with humanity. The result: a dramatic improvement in efficiency, fewer mistakes and delays, and far greater satisfaction with the work.

A second example comes from finance. Many team members spend their days producing detailed financial reports. In one case, a team of eight people sent out thirty-one reports every month. These ranged from five pages to over one hundred; the reports were typically thirty to forty pages long. We gave the team members an exercise in advance of a planned kaizen event: They were to stop sending those reports for a month, and see what happened. Would people validate that there was value in all those reports by asking for them?

At the end of the month, people had asked for only thirteen of the reports. Of those, some contained redundant information, so the team really only needed to send out ten reports a month to create value. It can be difficult to hear that so much of what you have worked hard to produce is not valued by people in the organization. But we urged the team to think of this as an opportunity. "Let's start with the ten reports. Let's use the extra time to focus on creating more value-added, insightful reports that look better, are shorter, and convey the information more effectively." Once they did that, they asked for feedback from the rest of the organization. They now had a much greater impact in the organization and received far more positive recognition by sending out fewer and better reports.

Our third example shows how critical it is that the people actually doing the work be the ones to redesign the process. We were laying out the machine shop for our spare parts value stream at PCMC in Green

Bay, Wisconsin. Ten of our divisional presidents focused for the better part of a week on how we could improve the value stream: getting spare parts orders entered, completed, and shipped to customers. They used their business experience to analyze the problem thoroughly, ran detailed routings for all the different parts we had to create, and put together a comprehensive plan. We looked at the plan a month later and realized that while it was great conceptually, it wasn't going to work in practice.

We tried again. The value stream had just picked its own leadership team. The leaders met in a weeklong kaizen event to lay out how they thought the business should operate. They looked at a number of different things, including different ways of utilizing manufacturing and office space. After about a month, we realized what we were discussing was going to be a challenge to implement, and we weren't respecting our team members in the ways that we should. So we had a third kaizen event with only two senior leaders and about ten people who were machine operators, forklift drivers, assemblers, people whose role was to "pick, pack, and ship," and people who put together work orders in the office. They took cardboard cutouts onto the floor of the factory and measured what they would need to bring different carts and forklifts through. They could see the different clearance issues and recognized that work from one area often flowed to another. Lighter parts would be easier to carry a farther distance. They looked at how many steps it took, how safe it was to have a forklift in an area, or whether it could come around the outside in a safer configuration.

This time, the solution worked beautifully. The way they laid it out is exactly how it remains today, five years later. It touches those team members' lives every day. They had wisdom that they were able to share to improve the process and create a meaningful, lasting, and more human process for everybody in that organization.

To reiterate: Lean is not really about waste elimination, it's about frustration elimination, removing obstacles that stand in the way of people being their best, that prevent us from having a joyful and meaningful experience. It's not about telling, it's about listening. It's about blending unique knowledge with collective wisdom. When we allow people and their teams to own the process, they can create better outcomes than any senior executive or group of consultants.

Asking the Right Questions . . . and Listening

As we teach in our leadership courses, there is often impact in asking the right question as opposed to finding the right answer. A question can be so thought-provoking that it takes us to a place we wouldn't otherwise get to. It is important to foster a culture in which we are open to asking questions in both directions. Many of our most memorable experiences and significant changes have resulted from questions people have asked us.

Our Guiding Principles of Leadership sessions usually open with leaders asking questions of the group: Where are we not living up to our vision? Where are the gaps? Where are the opportunities? What part of this is unclear? Questions like these have sparked much innovation and fresh thinking in our organization. These sessions always conclude with the opportunity for the participants in the room to ask questions of the senior leader. Such openness and transparency are what allow us to move forward. They create an environment where questioning the status quo is not only acceptable but encouraged, helping us to improve how we interact with each other every day.

Then we find avenues for people to share their experiences, so that others can learn and be inspired to change. We have people speak about how it makes them feel, whether it's an administrative assistant in St. Louis who says, "I can't believe that the leaders listened to me and championed my idea to the group and now we're going to implement it," or someone in Receiving who says, "Now that we've restructured the way that tractor-trailer trucks drop off at our facility, I'm done working at a reasonable time and can spend more time with my father at home."

We conclude with a story about Bonnie Peterson, an early winner in one of our recognition programs. She is responsible for quality control on aspects of our manufacturing operation at BW Papersystems in Phillips, Wisconsin. One line in our Safety Covenant says that we want every team member to "go home safe, well, and fulfilled each day." We organized an L^3 event to make that vision a reality for Bonnie. Throughout the event, she seemed to be struggling, as the changes were going to deeply affect her area.

In her report out at the end, Bonnie said, "You want to know how it made me feel? I've never heard so many four letter words in my life!" After some nervous laughter from the crowd, she said, "Everyone was saying, 'How do we make it *safe* for Bonnie? How do we make it *flow* for Bonnie? How do we make it *work* for Bonnie? How do we make it *good* for Bonnie? How do we make it *fast* for Bonnie?' Those are the four letter words I take away from this event: that everybody was focused on making it better for *me*. Even though it was challenging to hear some of the recommendations, it leaves me with a lasting sense of what this can be. I am so grateful to all of you."

Chapter 10

| Cultivating Responsible Freedom |

I magine your stereotypical IT programmer: Star Wars aficionado, on-line gamer at night, spends hours in front of a computer using acronyms you don't understand. All those things describe Ken Hoff, a veteran in our St. Louis corporate IT department. Ken would spend his lunch break working on screenplays and video projects he produced on the weekend. Then he would return to his 1s and 0s, wondering how meaningful it all really was. For years, many people knew about Ken's passions but also knew that work wasn't the place for them.

That was until his leader offered Ken an opportunity. The IT department was going to put together a carnival to raise funds for a local charity. Would Ken like to help with publicity? Ken could barely contain his excitement as he asked, "Can I do a video?"

The response came back quickly, "Of course! I was hoping you would."

Ken spent time on weekends and evenings writing scripts and pulling assistants from departments across the office. No one had acting experience, but they put together a five-minute video poking fun at the IT staff as carnival lovers. The link was sent to the whole organization—and it killed! Our IT staff were never bigger celebrities than they were that week. It was all anyone could talk about.

Where did this kind of talent come from? The truth is that talent of all kinds is lurking in our organizations—in the basement with IT, the back corner in accounting, and on the road with sales. We need to create a climate of freedom to unleash it.

Now imagine yourself as a machinist. If you don't know what a machinist does, imagine yourself getting a technical education and then a job working in the dingy recesses of a factory in northern Wisconsin. You apprentice there for a number of years, working on the same machine year in and year out. The factory is poorly lit, and there is oil and grease all over the floor. The machine itself has probably been on the earth as long as you have, constantly breaking down and needing coaxing to start up, like a beat-up old automobile. You're asked every day to use the machine to make parts from drawings that others have created, using steel that others have purchased. You can never do it fast enough or exactly the way that someone else envisioned it on their computer. Then people come to you with a vision that includes phrases like "empowerment" and "responsible freedom." You sit there wondering, "What the hell are they talking about?"

So many people have that same defeatist spirit of "How will I ever find an opportunity for empowerment in my role? How will it ever be different?" As we've discussed in the previous chapters, it can only be different if we're willing to change how we think about the process, and if we have leaders who are willing to lead by the code of the Leadership Checklist.

At Barry-Wehmiller, we've long used the word *empowerment*, but today it has become a meaningless buzzword in our society. We have come to realize that we need so much more than empowerment. Several years ago, we stumbled upon a term, *responsible freedom*, that has become central to how we describe our culture today. It came to us from the philosopher Peter Koestenbaum:

Taking personal responsibility for getting others to implement strategy is the leader's key polarity. It's the existential paradox of holding yourself 100 percent responsible for the fate of your organization, on the one hand, and assuming absolutely no responsibility for the choices made by other people, on the other hand. . . . You cannot choose for others. All you can do is inform them that you cannot choose for them. In most cases, that in itself will be a strong motivator for the people whom you want to cultivate. The leader's role is less to heal or to help than to enlarge the capacity for responsible freedom.[1]

Responsible freedom encapsulates two ideas: freedom, the opportunity to exercise personal choice, to have ownership of the work that you do and the decisions you make; and responsibility, ensuring that personal choice is exercised with care and concern for other people and the requirements of the organization. Whatever you call this concept—empowerment or responsible freedom—it is fundamental to driving fulfillment in any organization, and it requires two-way trust. Most people are merely compliant at work; their potential remains buried under layers of apathy and cynicism.

"Freedom from" and "Freedom to"

Both American society and capitalism are founded on the idea of freedom, but ironically, the institution in which we see the least amount of freedom is business. Indeed, some would say that businesses are the last bastions of command-and-control dictatorship. This is harmful to the well-being of people in the organization as well as to the organization itself. Without adequate freedom, people cannot contribute in the way that they are capable of, nor can they lead meaningful and fulfilling lives. It is therefore a moral imperative that we bring greater freedom into our work environments. As Dov Seidman puts it, "Freedom is a primal disposition and fundamental human right."[2]

There are two kinds of freedom: "freedom from" and "freedom to." Freedom *from* is about freeing people from excessive hierarchy, burdensome rules, stifling bureaucracy, and oppression. A command-and-control management style imposes many such curbs on freedom in the workplace. We should remove as many of these constraints as possible from every work environment. Many companies now use variations of a practice Commerce Bank (now part of TD Bank) pioneered a few years ago: "Kill a stupid rule." Employees were rewarded for pointing out rules that are silly, obsolete, or counterproductive.

Through our continuous-improvement events, we strive for what we call "just enough" structure. Once we define the right process, we allow for maximum responsible freedom within that process. We define "winning" and then give people the freedom to execute. Just enough structure means that we have established some guardrails but not imposed so many rules that they stifle individuality, personal judgment, innovation, or creativity.

While "freedom from" liberates individuals from oppressive rules, it does not by itself provide opportunities for them to express themselves. That is where "freedom *to*" comes in. People should have the freedom to innovate, experiment, and fail. But in the absence of shared values and a moral compass, "freedom to" can degenerate into self-serving anarchy. Dov Seidman says, "A handful of shared values is worth more than 1,000 rules." Any organization that wants to give a high degree of freedom to its people must first ensure that it has a rock-solid foundation of shared values and a shared vision for the future. With that foundation, individuals are freed and inspired to express themselves, extend trust, and contribute to the shared vision in extraordinary ways.

What Responsible Freedom Looks Like

At Barry-Wehmiller, responsible freedom entails three specific behaviors: sharing our gifts and talents, having a bias for action, and being accountable for the outcome. Sharing our gifts and talents is the freedom to offer who we truly are at work, to be the full human being that we are in the world. To have a bias for action is to not stand on the sidelines, but to be proactive and willing to grab the reins and take action toward the shared vision of the organization. Finally, responsible freedom means changing the essence of accountability: from a mechanism for assigning blame to an opportunity to work with others to create an organization that's better for all. To do this, we have to recognize that we are each stewards of the lives next to us and around us every day in our organizations. We are all accountable to each other. It's not only the executive leadership's responsibility or that of the person with the highest title in the organization.

We often say in our organization that we've paid people for their hands for years, but they would've gladly given us their heads and hearts for free if we'd only known how to ask. People are eager to do this in all organizations, but it really only works in an environment of responsible freedom.

Carol O'Neill sees responsible freedom as a key aspect of the Barry-Wehmiller culture:

At Barry-Wehmiller, you know what the goal is and how progress is measured at a high level for your business. You also know what the goal is for your function. You know what progress looks like, and you know what it feels like to succeed or not. These things give you that other element that is so crucial, which is the idea of responsible freedom. You give people the latitude to figure out how to do something, because they know the goal that we are all working toward. That is very empowering and satisfying. Obviously, everybody is wired differently, but people who thrive in an environment where the goals are clear but the path is not tend to be entrepreneurial, driven, motivated people. I want to know what we're aiming to do, but you take half the fun out of it if you tell me exactly how to get there.

Lighting Fires Versus Fighting Fires

The conventional wisdom is that the best leaders are firefighters, heroes who move mountains to accomplish the impossible. They walk in when a problem is already raging and miraculously engineer a desirable outcome. But through our journey of creating an environment of responsible freedom, we've learned that the best leaders rarely have to fight fires or come across as heroes dragging success from the jaws of failure. They take the time to develop an inspiring vision, design their business model to withstand external shocks, and build an environment of responsible freedom. It's always better to have every eye in the organization looking out for potential fires and opportunities for improvement than to have just one set of eyes looking. Such organizations avoid most fires in the first place.

If leadership isn't about fighting fires, what is it about? We believe it is about *lighting* fires. In our organization, we celebrate those who light fires in others by caring, listening, recognizing, and inspiring. Lighting fires has to begin within ourselves, with finding the light within who we are as human beings. Once we find that light, we can share it with others and encourage them to allow their fires to be lit and kindled and grown and shared with the organization.

To get the behaviors they seek, command-and-control leaders use extrinsic rewards like status or money or the threat of losing your job—the old "carrots and sticks" approach. As Daniel Pink pointed out in *Drive*, research over the last thirty to forty years has conclusively shown that intrinsic motivation trumps extrinsic motivation for work that requires creativity and out-of-the-box thinking. It is built on three primary factors: autonomy, mastery, and purpose[3]. Responsible freedom gives people autonomy to shape their own destiny and approach their work in ways that make sense for them. It also offers the opportunity to develop mastery, to shape their job, and to develop deep expertise. Finally, responsible freedom should always be exercised in service of the organization's shared purpose.

David Marquet, a former submarine commander in the US Navy, took command of one of the lowest-performing subs in the Navy and boldly proclaimed that it would become one of the top five submarines within a year. His crew looked at him and said, "No way! How are you going to do that for us?"

He said, "I'm not going to do it for you. I'm going to invite you to do it for yourselves." Within a year or two, he was leading the highest-rated ship in the Navy, not because of his own firefighting abilities, but because of his ability to light fires in others. What David did demonstrates the power of responsible freedom even in a traditionally command-and-control culture.[4]

Responsible Freedom Takes Trust

How do we get traditional leaders to accept the idea of responsible freedom? How do we get them to let go of the reins and offer some of their power, information, and responsibility to others? They need to connect with the organization's vision and develop deep trust with each other and with people throughout the organization. In our five-hour module on responsible freedom in the Leadership Fundamentals course, we spend more time discussing trust than anything else. Leaders at Barry-Wehmiller have to create an environment of trust as a prerequisite to creating the opportunity for responsible freedom for their team members.

Trust is an essential human attribute and virtue. Being both trusting and trustworthy are central to what it means to be a human being. Yet there is a huge trust deficit in our society today. There is a crisis of trust in government, in our educational system, in the health-care system and in the financial system. There is deep distrust toward companies and their leaders. Within companies, there is mutual distrust among employees, and among employees and customers, suppliers and leaders.

An environment lacking in trust fosters defensive, suspicious, insular, and fearful behavior, which depletes organizational energy and destroys creativity. A lack of trust imposes a burden of higher monitoring and legal costs. It makes companies sluggish, unresponsive, and uncaring. It sows the seeds for the eventual destruction of the organization.

Building trust requires constant, authentic communication. Communication is not just about words; it is also based on actions. Every action communicates something to employees. Too many companies say one thing and do another, breeding deep cynicism among employees over time. Like the barnacles that attach themselves to a ship's underside over time, this cynicism is very difficult for companies to remove.

To get trust, you have to freely give it. Leaders must start by trusting their people to use their own judgment and follow their own instincts rather than controlling them with too many directives and rules. High-trust businesses are built on respect and caring, not fear and anxiety. They exhibit high levels of teamwork, synergy, and cooperation. They are energetic, optimistic, can-do organizations that can overcome seemingly insurmountable odds. Trust within the company radiates out to all stakeholders, including customers, investors, partners, communities, government, and society as a whole. The company's reputation is enhanced, giving it a halo that allows it to attract ever-better employees, customers, suppliers, and investors—starting a virtuous cycle that builds over time to create a truly great company that generates tremendous value and well-being for society as a whole.

At Barry-Wehmiller, we use an approach for building trust that we call CCCI: compassion, competence, consistency, and integrity.

Compassion: We care about the concerns of others, and we demonstrate that care through our ability to listen, to take others' perceptions into account, and to have empathy.

Competence: We can perform the tasks that we are asked to complete. That includes technical competence and leadership competence: Are we competent at the Leadership Checklist items that define the culture we're in?

Consistency: People feel they will receive a consistent reaction whether they come with a question today or tomorrow.

Integrity: We do what we say we will do, and it's in alignment with the stated values, vision, and direction of our organization.

The CCCI approach is particularly useful in how we form and think about teams. Trust is essential for team development. For a team to continue to develop, the trust must not just be between the leader and the associates, it needs to be between every individual on the team. These areas form a diagnostic for evaluating how to take a team from one level of trust to the next.

Unleashing Latent Potential

At Barry-Wehmiller, we don't simply put out a suggestion box and ask for anonymous suggestions. The most important part of any suggestion program is feedback to the person who offered the idea. We owe people the respect to respond to them about the progress, status, and evaluation of their ideas. Of course, not all ideas can be implemented. We find that when we provide feedback publicly, personally, and with rigor, we get more ideas and the quality is higher.

We give people the opportunity to take ownership in areas that they are truly passionate about and in which they are willing to step up and lead. We return to our story of the machinist in northern Wisconsin. Fortunately, this machinist has a leader who has embarked on a personal journey of building responsible freedom. His name is George Senn, and he is a son of the north woods who has lived there his entire life, becoming first an apprentice and then a master machinist. Like others before him, he was promoted to supervisor because he was the best machinist at the time. Having worked at the factory for twenty-five years, he knows the people on his team well. He knows that in the back of the building, where it's dingy and dark and challenging, people don't know how to be inspired and offer their best gifts. But he is willing to embrace the awesome responsibility of leadership; he is willing to leave behind a command-and-control structure that comes so naturally to him and change to a different way of leadership—that of lighting fires in others.

When we first began our cultural journey at BW Papersystems in Phillips, we made some changes that had a big impact. The customer-service team was having a lot of fun with their games and creating a sense of winning. We had just developed our Guiding Principles of Leadership and were beginning to get some early adopters on board. George loved this new way of leading and asked for advice on how to implement it in the machine shop there.

The machine shop was a tough place to work. Dan Kundinger was a machinist who joined in some of the first cultural sessions. He suffered a lot of ribbing from his colleagues when he came back. "Did you drink the Kool-Aid?" This was a team that was very resistant to change, very slow to accept this new culture.

George asked Rhonda Spencer, "How can we create this kind of culture in the machine shop?"

The journey was so new, she didn't have an answer for him. He walked her through the area, and she thought, "It looks like the work at the post office. No matter how much you get done today, there is always a stack of packages [in this case, drawings of parts to be machined] waiting. You only get feedback on the things that go wrong—parts with errors or ones that are late—never on what went right. You just chug away every day and never know when you go home at night if you won—there's no scoreboard to tell you what a good day's work looks like. In that environment, it's hard to be inspired, it's hard to feel connected to the big picture."

George did do some things to create a "Team Machine Shop" culture and build some personal bonds among the team, but without the tools to fix the core problems, those efforts didn't go very far. Once we started our Lean journey, George had the tools to begin to change the way the machine shop worked. He could put more control in the hands of the team members, change the way priorities were set, and create better lines of communication with the engineers and planners upstream and the assemblers downstream. That is when the culture truly began to change.

After completing our process-improvement training, George began to interact with his team differently. He began to ask for the benefit of everyone's head, heart, and hands. We produce more than 10,000 discrete parts in that one machine shop in northern Wisconsin each year to help our customers keep their machines running smoothly and often operate multiple shifts. There was a wide disparity of information and understanding as to how to best set up each part on a machine and run it. That disparity led to many issues that customers and the organization could see, such as when we couldn't produce a part on a given shift because the manufacturing order specifically said, "Have Ted do this one." It was demoralizing to the associates: They wanted to meet the customer need, take ownership of the process, and get the parts and products out to our customers, but they didn't have that opportunity because we lacked an environment of responsible freedom.

George invited everyone to fill out a one-page setup sheet on each part they produced. They would take pictures of the setup and describe the tools and the settings, sharing the wisdom of their fifteen or twenty or thirty years of putting that part together. This way, anyone could take that sheet and set up the machine and be effective in doing what was needed for the customer. It is not a standard practice in these kinds of shops to share setup sheets. A lot of people said, "George, this will never work. You're asking people to reduce their own job security by offering what's inside their head to others. People will be threatened by this; they'll never participate."

George said, "I think I can inspire people to participate."

They set a goal to create 7,000 setup sheets within nine months.

Within the first year, George's group had produced over 10,000 setup sheets. We are now at over 12,000 setup sheets. Now they're able to meet any demand and win each day. That is the power of an environment of responsible freedom. Quality improved by a factor of three, as measured by the number of errors or defined rework that they had to do.

George's new style of leadership has had a ripple effect throughout the organization. One of the machining groups in George's area is run by Lance Johnson, who was inspired to take the Leadership Fundamentals course and create an environment of responsible freedom in his group. Lance and two machinists operated a laser cutter—probably the most technically complex machine in the entire building, and the one most frequently down for maintenance. We needed to look into replacing the machine.

Both George and Lance knew that one of our business priorities is to be intensely diligent about capital expenditures. We continually challenge ourselves to ensure the sustainability of our business model and make the right decisions to build in house or subcontract to local vendors. These purchases are so important that for more than a decade every purchase order for a machine tool had to be personally approved by me. In 2011, I empowered a team to utilize the Lean tools of continuous improvement to design a new process that would put the decision-making power in the hands of our people.

Lance took the responsible freedom to work with his team and request approval for the largest machine purchase in the facility's history with Barry-Wehmiller. "I didn't know it would be approved, but I said 'Let's go for it!' So our team went into homework mode. We wanted to prove to senior leadership that we could make the right decision, so we applied the 'listen, empower, and trust' triangle from Barry-Wehmiller University."

Lance's team started using their downtime and even weekends to research all the possible purchases that would fulfill their needs. "I've bought a house in my life, I've bought vehicles, but I never had a chance to buy capital equipment. I started doing homework on what's good about lasers. We were committed to getting it right—not for some corporate purchasing group, but for us, for our livelihoods."

After they received initial approval for the purchase, Lance's team reacted with enthusiasm: "You could see them start to beam when we asked, 'What do you think?' It was a big step for them."

Lance and Derek, the machine operator, located a piece of equipment for sale about a two-hour drive away. The seller was flabbergasted when they arrived to check out the machine because all the other interested buyers had sent their purchasing managers. Lance remembers, "We walked in with a quarter of a million dollar PO in hand, and I was shaking when I walked out. Derek crawled all over the machine. He said, 'I need some more information about whether this will have the maintenance capabilities that we need before we can agree to buy it.' I think the guy was pretty surprised."

Three months later, they oversaw the installation of the machine and utilized Lean tools to create new processes that fully utilized all the machine's features. An outside trainer came in to prep the team and remarked, "They could be doing my job! They already know everything."

The laser cutter is now a prime tour stop for customers and guests and has become a symbol of what is possible in an environment of responsible freedom. In 2014, a delegation from Harvard Business School led by Professor Amy Cuddy came to the factory, and Lance's team stood out as the most memorable tour stop. Amy remarked, "We don't even allow white-collar workers to pick out their own computers, but here is an example of passionate associates taking ownership of their work."

Let Freedom Flow

In the end, the person who was most impacted by the entire experience was George himself. Without Lean making real changes to the work of the machine shop, the team members would never have had the trust to engage in the setup process. Without responsible freedom, Lance and his laser team would never have selected their own machine.

George is an example of a leader whose heart was always in the right place, he just didn't know how to lead in this way. He had taken a risk to try to lead differently, and in the end he found a far greater connection with his team and a greater sense of accomplishment, in terms not only of what they had accomplished but of how they did it together. This is the promise for any leader. Being willing to trust in others, not just loosen but throw away the reins, and invite responsible freedom will not only transform your business; it will also affect the person you are at work and at home.

George is so excited about what his team continues to accomplish that he goes out of his way to share frequent updates with the organization. Every quarter, additional setup sheets are completed, improved, and refined, and quality and performance continue to increase in his team.

By creating an environment of responsible freedom, we show real respect for the true craftsmen and craftswomen in our organizations, often for the first time. That is especially true in manufacturing, where we've stereotyped groups and set them up to experience process-driven frustration. The ability to express the creativity and artistry and crafts-manship of what people do has been lost in the detailed processes and structures we've put them in. But it's true in so many other areas in our organization as well. There can be just as much artistry and craftsman-ship in how we tie together financial information and present and share it with other people in inspiring and innovative ways. The common denominator is responsible freedom.

Chapter 11

| Recognition and Celebration |

Afew years ago, I was at a football game, watching the Green Bay Packers play. The quarterback Brett Favre threw a long pass into the end zone. The receiver caught the ball, jubilantly spiked it, and then, following a long-standing tradition at Lambeau Field, did the exuberant "Lambeau leap." He jumped into the stands to soak in the adulation of fans, who caught him, patted him on the back, and dropped him back on the field.

It made me think, "He is an incredibly gifted receiver who worked hard to be in a position to make that catch. It was a great catch, a catch that few people could have made, but the truth is that he didn't do it alone. A lot of people did the right thing to put him in a position to make that great catch."

Just once, I'd like to see the receiver set the ball down, run back to the line of scrimmage, help a lineman up off the ground (after removing someone weighing 300 pounds who has been lying on top of him), and say, "Great block! I would never have gotten open if it wasn't for that block." He should go back to the quarterback and say, "Brilliant pass, right where I expected it to be!" When he returns to the sideline, he should say to the coach, "Thanks for designing that play pattern, it allowed me to be open. The other team really didn't see it coming!'"

This idea became the basis for our High Five award, which recognizes those who enable others to succeed. For example, when a salesperson receives an order, she can go back into the organization and recognize the people who made the blocks, created the play patterns, and threw the pass that allowed her to be successful. Anyone can nominate a colleague who they feel went out of their way to help them be successful. I send a letter to their family celebrating the recognition, and they receive a simple gift such as dinner for two or tickets to a local event. More than the gift, they feel deeply touched by the letter and by the fact that their peers recognize their goodness.

Our Most Abundant Resource

People need to feel personally significant at work—to feel that they make a valuable contribution. One of the items in our Leadership Checklist is "I recognize and celebrate the greatness in others." Our many recognition programs provide a framework and opportunities to identify and celebrate team members who exemplify our definition of true success. It is one of the more unique aspects of Barry-Wehmiller's culture.

In most organizations, people do the right thing most of the time, but most communication is about the things that go wrong. In a culture like ours that's focused on continuous improvement, you could spend so much time looking for gaps or issues or challenges that you forget to stop and celebrate successes along the way. I was taught long ago that if more than half of your communication with any individual is negative, it's an oppressive relationship. So we make a conscious effort to fill our airwaves with goodness.

We introduced our Guiding Principles of Leadership SSR Award in Chapter 4. It remains our flagship recognition program, where team members nominate their peers for being outstanding examples of our

GPL culture. We give out versions of this award in our businesses around the world. Recipients are decided not by popular vote, but by the quality of what is written in the nominations. Team members put a huge amount of effort into capturing the unique goodness of their peers. We get dozens of nominations for every award; even those who aren't selected get a copy of what was written about them, which is deeply meaningful to them.

The awards are presented in organization-wide celebrations, with team members coming out in crowds to experience it. It is a joy to see the winner's face when the result is announced, but just as joyful to watch the faces of the crowd—smiling, crying, applauding, nodding in approval to say, "Yes, she really deserves it!" People line up to shake hands with the winner, who feels like a celebrity.

Rhonda Spencer says, "For me, to be in the crowd at one of these events is to be overwhelmed with a sense of gratitude for the good things in life. I feel joy for the winner, pride for the family who is standing alongside the winner, gratitude for those in the organization who have planned this amazing celebration for their peer, and amazement at this culture we've created."

The recipient gets to drive a unique convertible for a week, taking their "trophy" around town. The typical response is that their neighbors come out of the house to see if they've had a midlife crisis! People stop them at gas stations to ask about the car. They take the car to remote locales for their family to see it. Each time, the recipient has an opportunity to say, "The people at work recognized me for my leadership . . ." Most often what they hear in return is "I wish I worked at a place like that."

The Cultural Foundation

When we launched the Guiding Principles of Leadership award program in Phillips, Wisconsin, we found an organization in which people were starved for recognition. Many businesses we buy were built by entrepreneurs who had become very distrustful as the business entered difficult times. In such environments, recognition and celebration were rare.

When we went into this organization and introduced the GPL SSR Award program, it wasn't well received at first. It meant a lot to the winner, but what then rippled out across the organization could only be called jealousy. As we thought about the climate we were walking into, we understood why. What would you expect if you went into a group of starving people and served just one person a Thanksgiving feast? We realized that we needed to create an organizational culture in which recognition and celebration are plentiful.

Since then, we have indeed made recognition and celebration our most abundant resource. When people ask, "Why is there an award for customer service, but not one for finance?" we say, "Yes, of course we should have an award in finance. Let's define what makes a great finance team member and recognize and celebrate that." It's not just leaders doing the recognizing; everyone everywhere starts looking for the goodness in other people and holding it up.

The more we recognize and celebrate, the more people experience not only how good it feels to be on the receiving end but also how good it feels to be on the giving end. The person who gives a great recognition gains as much or more from it than the person who receives it. Recognition creates enormous positive energy in the organization. Ours has become a company of givers, of people constantly looking for opportunities to do something good for someone else.

Our recognitions run the gamut from the grand celebration—the GPL SSR Award being our grandest—to the simple compliment. When this kind of thing is done well, it can be a defining moment in a person's life, because people need to feel that they matter. In this business of encouraging the heart, we expect our leaders to go first and set an example. Paraphrasing Gandhi, we say to them, "Be the change you want to see in the organization." Once they start the ball rolling, others soon follow.

Business consultant Marcus Buckingham talks about "the simple, charming secrets of extraordinary people. In the corners of every big company that we've studied, there are hundreds or thousands of them toiling away in relative obscurity. If you find them and shine a light on them, they will point the company's way to the future."[1] We continually shine a light into every corner of our organization, searching for goodness, those individuals who are "toiling away in relative obscurity." When we find them, we hold up their goodness for all to see and applaud and be inspired by. We're building a culture in which everyone, everywhere, is delighted to recognize others and celebrate them as beacons of goodness.

Why Recognition and Celebration Are Critical

Why we do anything in our culture is always important, and recognition and celebration are no exception. Most companies look for a return on their investment in everything they do. If they recognize and celebrate people, it is to get better engagement and thus more productivity out of them. We believe that if you recognize and celebrate people to get more out of them, they're going to know it and feel it. We do it simply because it's the right thing to do; it's the way we are called to treat people, and the way that we would like to be treated ourselves. It's *never* to get more out of people. We recognize and celebrate people simply to *let them know that they matter*. Knowing that their colleagues understand their work and value it is deeply meaningful to them.

Recognition and celebration engage people's hearts and minds. Research shows that there is a strong correlation between these two statements: "I feel I am contributing to my company's mission" and "This company gives enough recognition for work that's well done."[2] It's not just the grand celebration of the GPL SSR Award; everyday expressions of appreciation that are genuine, heartfelt, and meaningful give people energy and let them know when they go home every day that they matter. We want our people to realize that small appreciations that are well expressed and genuine have a ripple effect that is more powerful than they might realize.

We don't assume that this will happen by accident. Everything we do in our culture that we think is important, we support systematically. We teach people how to do it well, put programs in place to support it, and support the everyday practice of it. We're pretty good at learning from ourselves and our own experiences. When you interview someone who has been nominated by their peers for being a great example of leadership, you get a window into understanding what people in the organization value, what's going right, and how the best people in our organization operate in their daily work. We capture that learning and make it part of what we teach others.

Our awards help people become even better leaders. Jay Dietz has found that in virtually every case, the GPL Award "grew the individual into a greater leader." These individuals exemplify even better what people recognized in them, because they feel challenged and encouraged to live up to what their colleagues said about them. It is a kind of identity refreshment and reinforcement.

Take the case of Richard Pike, an assembler and machine tester at Hayssen Flexible Systems in South Carolina and one of the first GPL SSR Award winners in that plant. A year after he won, I ran into him and asked him, "So, Richard, what does it feel like to have been a GPL Award winner?"

Richard replied, "I didn't think I deserved it. It really changed me to read all of those nominations and see what people thought about me. I had no idea that people saw me that way. Now, a year later, I think about what they said, *and I come in every day and try to be the person they think I am.*"

What We Recognize and Celebrate

Here's the cutting edge of common sense: organizations should recognize and celebrate the things they want more of. In our course on recognition and celebration, we teach that there are many things we can recognize. The first question we ask people to consider is whether a behavior could be described as firefighting or fire lighting. Many organizations recognize firefighting behaviors: someone who saved the day in a heroic way. We tell the story in our class about the time our CIO Craig Hergenroether's daughter was working in another organization, and she said, "We're taking our IT team to happy hour tonight because we got this big e-mail virus, but they did a great job cleaning it up."

Our CIO thought, "We never got the virus. We put all the disciplines and practices in place to ensure that we never got it. Shouldn't we celebrate that?"

What we choose to hold up and celebrate gets emulated. Therefore it is important to consider how those decisions impact the culture. Instead of firefighting behaviors, we recognize and celebrate sustained excellence: people who consistently distinguish themselves through their actions. We celebrate people who do their jobs very well every day with little drama. Craig, the CIO, took his team out to happy hour and said, "Congratulations, we did not get the e-mail virus that took out most of the companies in St. Louis and Tampa Bay."

We also recognize and celebrate exemplary behaviors (the manner of acting/conducting oneself), innovative processes (courses of action intended to achieve results), exceptionally positive outcomes (end results of behaviors or actions), and tangible achievements.

How We Recognize and Celebrate

To recognize is "to acknowledge, to grant credentials to." To celebrate is to "assign great social importance to." Whether large scale or intimate, celebrations increase feelings of belonging and build greater team spirit. But just saying "Thanks, buddy" is not enough. We teach people to craft recognition in a meaningful way that allows recipients to see that it's genuine. It's a skill that can be taught and a culture that can be grown.

Our awards don't have a monetary component, because we find that money is not as memorable or impactful. Incentive compensation is separate from recognition and celebration. We use incentive compensation to align the objectives of individuals with the goals of the organization so that when they win, they're also creating value for the organization.

We strive to make our recognitions and celebrations personal, memorable, creative, sincere, timely, proportionate, significant, and meaningful. Timely means that recognition should happen as close to the event as possible. Creativity is important, so people know you thought about it and did something special and unique. Recognition should be personal; even within big celebrations, there should always be something that lets individuals know that this is about them and is not just a standard corporate event.

Recently at our headquarters in St. Louis, Tim Sullivan, group president, was recognized as a winner of the GPL SSR Award. Many things were written and said about the business success that he has helped create and the opportunities he's given people, but many more comments were about his style and how he leads. When Tim was asked about what had meant the most to him about the celebration, he said it was the effort that people had put into making the celebration special and unique for him. They did a "mad science" theme with Tim's wife, Mary, dressed up in a white lab coat, a cap, and a mask. The surprise of having his family there, doing something potentially embarrassing in front of the whole company to celebrate him, was very special. For all the success that Tim has enjoyed through his career, this was particularly meaningful. He said, "It means so much to me that the team here in St. Louis would put this kind of effort into celebrating me."

When Diana Hill from our IT support team was selected to receive the GPL SSR Award, her leader, chief technical officer Robert Richards, was part of planning the celebration. In addition to getting to drive the SSR, Robert gave her a pink catcher's mitt mounted on a stand that he had crafted in his garage. He said, "Everything in this department goes through your hands, and you never drop the ball." What Robert said to her that day was, "I see what you do around here and I value it. You make a difference. *You matter.*" What more does anyone want to hear from their leader?

Significance is something we struggled with in the beginning. We had a salesperson who compared every order he received to the legendary Ice Bowl, considered the greatest football game ever played. One time he was celebrating an order—"It was the Ice Bowl!"—and going on about it until his leader said to him, "You know, your team needs to get an order like that every week to meet your goal. Every single order can't be the Ice Bowl." The goal is to be proportionate to the accomplishment and significant for the person who made it happen. If we exaggerate people's accomplishments, the recognition becomes meaningless.

Most of our awards are based on peer nominations. They are not popularity contests. The process challenges people to sit down and write things about their coworkers that they may never have taken the time to say to them. Whether people win or not, reading what people wrote about them creates a real sense of meaning around the awards. Often, people who are nominated are also interviewed. It allows us to really dig into the good things that are going on in the organization and expand on them, and also helps others understand more deeply what makes that person tick.

One of our practices that has the most impact is sending letters to people's homes. It means so much to people for their parents or spouse or children to know about the contribution that they're making and the impact they have on their colleagues. As part of the High Five celebration of Mike Wilwerth, a field service leader at Hayssen Flexible Systems, I sent a letter to his wife. Afterward, he told us, "I was never sure my wife really understood what I do, or cared that much, but she had a whole new appreciation for the impact that I have on the organization when she saw this letter. She was really proud, and that meant a lot to me."

Polo Juangorena is a member of our BW Papersystems sales organization in Latin America. He has done a lot to contribute to the success of that business through the orders he's closed. To recognize his contributions, I sent his wife a letter and a bouquet of flowers. I wrote, "We want to share our pride and gratitude for everything that Polo has accomplished." Fifteen years later, at an anniversary celebration of the acquisition, Polo got up and talked about that letter. After all the success he had and all the recognition he had received, the letter still stood out. He talked about how meaningful it was to have that letter celebrating him sent to his wife—and the bouquet of flowers thanking her for all the support that she gives him so that he can be on the road succeeding for us.

Making It Safe to Care

When we teach recognition and celebration in our Leadership Fundamentals course in BWU, we get to a point where it all seems like rainbows and unicorns. The giver feels great, the recipient feels great, and we all go on our merry way, right? But if it was so obvious, it would be much more prevalent in businesses today. So we ask people, "What holds you back?" The typical responses:

◇ Why would I thank someone for just doing their job? That's what they get paid to do.
◇ I say "Thanks" to people all the time, and "Good work." Isn't that enough?
◇ It makes people uncomfortable to be recognized in public.
◇ You don't want to seem like you are sucking up.
◇ It could create a problem if you need to reprimand them later.

Sometimes people feel uncomfortable receiving recognition because they've never had it before and it doesn't feel natural or right to them. Many people have been taught that emotion has no place in business, that successful people leave it out, and that brutal honesty is the only way.

We want to make it safe for people to care and to express caring. We bring emotion into business in a constructive way. It seems so obvious and easy to recognize people, and in most cases it costs very little. Some people worry that if you over-recognize something, it will lose its meaning. We teach people how to do it in a meaningful way so that nothing is ever diminished by recognizing and celebrating someone.

In a Lean culture, some people think that recognizing individuals could be detrimental to the team. These people have a more socialistic view of recognition and celebration; they believe that holding up one individual in a team environment creates animosity. That can happen, but it doesn't mean that the idea is wrong, just its implementation. We hold up individuals because that's the only way to let them know they matter. We also have combined team and individual awards. Often, when we hold up individuals, they voluntarily share the recognition with the team that helped make them successful.

It takes time and effort to put together a great celebration. It's not just thinking about what to say and tracking down parents' addresses and those kinds of things. It's also taking the emotional risk that people will receive it with the intent with which you give it. People are often afraid to put themselves out there and take that risk.

One day I got into a conversation with the leadership team at one of our plants about culture and the challenge of saying "thank you" and recognizing people. Brett Dexheimer, now the VP of operations at Thiele, told me about someone in the plant named Bruce. The plant had experienced a labor stoppage a few years earlier. It was a pretty tense standoff, with strikers banging on the president's car as it came through the picket line. Bruce was a passionate union member and was at the front of the group banging on the car. The strike eventually got settled, and everybody came back to work.

A project manager told Brett, "I've been working on a project with Bruce. We were struggling to get this machine to run for a customer checkout, and we were all frustrated—the engineer, the project manager, and Bruce, who was there as the test team member on the project. I finally said, 'OK, let's give it a rest. We're all tired, it's getting late. We'll come back tomorrow and get a fresh start.' Bruce said, 'Would you mind if I stayed? I want to try a few things. Maybe I can have it working for you guys in the morning.' Now, that's what I consider true leadership."

Brett said to me, "I have seen a real change in Bruce since we had all our struggles. It was all I could muster a while back to pull Bruce aside at the end of the day as he was walking out the door and say, 'Hey, Bruce, I appreciate the leadership you're showing, the contribution you're making. I just want to thank you for it.'"

I said, "Why don't we get Bruce in here? Ask him if he remembers that. This is part of our learning and the evolution of our journey." Bruce came in and stood against the wall awkwardly as they related the story to him. I asked him if he remembered when Brett gave him that compliment. It had been about six months.

Bruce said, "Do I remember? Do you know what it's like when the big boss pulls you aside and says something like that to you? I thought about it all the way home in my truck, and I thought about it all the way back the next day. I still think about it nearly every day."

Within any organization, there are people who respond better to particular kinds of recognition, whether it's one-on-one, a more private gesture, or the grand celebration. But people's need to feel a sense of belonging, to feel that they matter, is the same across organizations and around the world. In the United Kingdom, people told us that this kind of recognition wouldn't work, because their culture was different. Such statements are symptoms of cultures where celebration is rare. As we were closing our most recent acquisition in Italy, they too were saying, "We don't think that's going to work in our culture." Simon Lagoe, who runs our Hayssen Flexible Systems operation in the UK, grinned and said to them, "Well, guys, I have to tell you something. We used to say it's because we're British, but the fact is we just didn't want to do it. But it works for us the same as it works anywhere else. Just try it."

The Freedom to Recognize and Celebrate

Many people worried that our recognition programs would be cut when we implemented furloughs and various kinds of austerity measures during the 2009 downturn. A recognition program is often one of the first things that organizations cut when they're trying to save money, because it is seen as frivolous. But if you look at the actual cost of our GPL SSR Award program, it's not that much while the lasting power it has is enormous. In the economic downturn, we did scale the celebrations back so that they were less lavish and appropriate to the times we were going through, but we didn't reduce them. People became highly creative and came up with cost-effective ideas that we continued to use later on.

In our culture now, responsible freedom has come together with recognition and celebration in gratifying ways. Our people know that anyone can create an award; it doesn't have to come from corporate. Remember George Senn, the leader in the machine shop in Phillips? The machine shop had a tough, old-school culture, but George is a leader with heart, and he wanted to make a difference. After he completed Leadership Fundamentals and learned about recognition and celebration, he lost a team member named Dennis Wilson to a heart attack. George decided to launch a memorial award in honor of Dennis, given by machine shop team members to a fellow team member who exemplifies what Dennis stood for as one of the first leaders on the continuous-improvement journey. The Dennis Wilson Memorial Award is now presented every six months. When this happened we knew that our drive to make recognition and celebration central to our culture was working; it is now part of the organizational fabric, and people have taken ownership of it.

Chapter 12

| Educating Leaders |

M ike Davis of our PneumaticScaleAngelus division is emblematic of the next generation of leaders within Barry-Wehmiller: a young, talented engineer in a quickly changing and growing organization. Given the opportunity, it was natural for him to sign up for a class called Leadership Fundamentals. He described his motivation as exactly what you'd expect. "I want to learn some skills to become a better leader." Leadership Fundamentals, however, is not designed to impart skills. It is designed to be a transformative experience that inspires people to truly embrace the awesome responsibility of leadership. Inspiring profound, personal change calls for an entirely different approach to education. Here is how Mike described his experience:

> As the class went on, I changed my goal from "How can I better myself?" to "How can I help better those around me?" As a leader, and ultimately a mentor, you have the responsibility and privilege to grow those around you and help them become their absolute best. I credit my Barry-Wehmiller University experiences with helping me become a more approachable, unreserved person. I used to hold back and act more like a filter. I realized that's not necessarily the best thing to do. People want feedback. They want to know what's going on. The class taught me the importance of letting people know how I feel and how to show my appreciation for the work they do. Now

I'm building personal relationships with others. I'm leading people, not managing them. I'm partnering with others as a mentor. These things all build the trust that you must have with your team members and partners. The experiences at BWU have meant a tremendous amount to me. Every day I'm calling on those experiences, whether it's in the workplace, at home, or even the grocery store. You have the chance to impact people each and every day, and what you do with those opportunities makes you who you are. That's the great thing about Leadership Fundamentals. It's not just related to your work environment. I took a lot of what I learned and correlated it to my personal life and especially in my relationship with my wife. Now I can open up more with her about what's happening in my life at work and what I'm feeling, and I think our relationship has grown because of that. It's true what they taught us: You're making a profound behavioral change, and you can't do that in just one part of your life.

The University

The journey to creating Barry-Wehmiller University to embed our unique take on leadership and culture into the organization for the long term started a few years before we formally launched the university in 2008.

Remember Steve Kreimer and the question he posed about how to bring the culture statement that we have on our walls into behaviors for our leaders? At the time, we were a few years into the idea of combining the tools of Lean with our Guiding Principles of Leadership. Our embedded Lean team leaders in our divisions had a meeting during which I asked them, "What is the number-one thing you need to be successful in bringing about this fusion between Lean tools and the Guiding Principles of Leadership?"

Their response was, "We really need leadership training." So I came back and challenged our team with "How can we create leadership education within this organization?"

In true Barry-Wehmiller team style, we ran a visioning session. We brought together a cross-functional group of people to talk about what teaching leadership within Barry-Wehmiller could look like. We wrote a very short vision statement with only two bullets:

The first one says that the purpose of Barry-Wehmiller University is to develop an integrated, inspirational, and sustainable way of living our vision. Those three words—integrated, inspirational, and sustainable—are at the heart of what BWU is about. It's very important to us that people feel like the things we talk about within BWU are fully integrated into our everyday actions, into every Lean event, into each meeting, into our daily interactions, and that it's always inspirational. It also needs to be sustainable; if we do this right, it will live beyond any leader's time. We need to be able to transfer the things that we so strongly believe in to people across the organization.

The second is our belief that we can use the power of business to dramatically impact the world in a positive way. We believe deeply in the ripple effect of leadership. We think that if we give people tools that enable them to use their gifts and talents each day, they will go home more fulfilled and interact with their families and communities and the world as people who are ready to face any challenge. If people felt more fulfilled by the work they do, they would be better equipped to handle life challenges like marriage and parenting. If every business did this, we could transform the world.

Core Philosophies

In that same meeting, we also decided on three principles that we've stuck with. The first concerned *what* we would teach: we wouldn't teach content from other sources. We decided that we would develop our own material because we wanted it to be distinctively Barry-Wehmiller, evocative of our unique worldview that you couldn't get anywhere else.

The second was about *who* would teach. We decided that every professor would be a team member of Barry-Wehmiller rather than someone we hired from the outside. We would create a career milestone for people to be able to share their wisdom and stories with their peers. We felt that there was tremendous authenticity in the stories they could share, something that external trainers using off-the-shelf content could not give us.

Third, we decided that the process of *how* we taught had to be inspirational and transformational from the beginning.

We recognize that Barry-Wehmiller University is one component of an overall cultural strategy. BWU provides the skills and behaviors that allow people to participate and grow within our people-centric culture. But we don't achieve cultural transformation just by putting people in the classroom; it's a component that lies alongside other change processes. Without the continuous-improvement journey, without the recognition and celebration, without individual and team coaching, the training would not be as relevant or impactful. We know that people need to experience these things to truly learn them.

Like with everything else we do, BWU is not about getting more out of people or enhancing performance. It is not about improving productivity, and we don't expect a particular return on investment. We go to great lengths to make sure that people understand that Barry-Wehmiller

University exists to enhance their ability to touch people's lives and equip them to be successful with others both inside and outside Barry-Wehmiller. We don't draw a line between behaviors within the work-place and how people can apply them at home. What surprises participants is that we encourage telling stories about our home lives as much as we talk about the things we do in our leadership roles at work.

Our associates teach. When we decided to go down this path, we didn't know if we were fully equipped for what that would mean, and if we could meet the challenge that we were giving people by asking them to stand up and teach their peers. It's a tremendous opportunity, but also a tremendous challenge. How do you inspire people to tell their stories? How do you teach them how to facilitate?

We developed a one-week Professor Training program through which we've now taught close to 200 people, from inside and outside Barry-Wehmiller, to be professors in our style. It's centered around three big ideas. The first is that your job as a professor is to impart insight, which is different than imparting information. Second, your job is to create the perfect environment for learning. And, third, you have to inspire change. That requires that you think about every detail, such as the room dynamic, the disclosures you offer to people, and the config-uration people sit in. We don't do a lot of "awareness training"; we want people to be intensely impacted by their experience so that it leads to significant behavior change. For that reason, our shortest classes run three days, while long classes require an investment of two to three weeks. We want people to think differently about themselves and about their work, and we push them incredibly hard to be reflective in that process.

Feed the Hungry

A question I frequently get after speeches is, "What do you do about the people who don't get it?"

My response is frustrating to some: "We don't focus on the people who don't get it. We focus on those who do." This philosophy is also reflected in how we fill our classes at BWU. Our unofficial mantra is "Feed the hungry." *None* of our training is mandatory or automatic; everyone who takes a course must go through an application process.

We are not in the conversion business; we want all participants to be intrinsically motivated. We focus on where we can have the most impact. If you're intrinsically motivated, you acquire knowledge better, you retain knowledge better, and you apply that knowledge more often and with greater effect. Considering our professor model and that we often have people up in front of the room who are teaching for the first time, we want to provide them with an audience that is primed and eager to learn and grow. We want the experience to be good for everyone. We believe that if the people in our classes are well fed with insights, they will go out and stimulate more hunger in the organization, and then we can feed those hungry people.

You can also think about it in terms of a marketing adoption curve. Just as people line up outside Apple stores waiting for the latest iPhone, we have people lined up when we roll out a new class. It doesn't matter what the class is about, they are excited to be a part of it. We nourish those hungry people.

A common practice in our divisional course work is to do a report out at the end of a class. Participants are asked to invite a person—it could be their leader or somebody else whom they feel the class would be great for—and share their experience with that person. They don't try to teach the content, but try to convey a sense of what it was like for them to progress through the class.

People share their personal stories using skits, videos, and other creative ways. Hearing those stories firsthand creates a whole new cycle of demand, so that those next people become really excited about the opportunity to invest three days or three weeks in that learning opportunity.

Leadership education is not reserved for people with titles. We focus on people who want to take the next step in their leadership journey, no matter what their official title or role is. We feel that the benefit of doing that outweighs the value of bringing in people who theoretically have more influence but won't necessarily make the requisite changes. Some people would prefer that we take entire teams, or that we start with the most senior leaders and work our way down the organizational chart. It's uncomfortable for some leaders when members of their team go through Leadership Fundamentals before they do. But we are clear: we want people to make a personal choice to embark on this journey when they're ready to do so, regardless of their current position.

Our model is based on heavy doses of disclosure and people offering up their stories. At the beginning of every Leadership Fundamentals class, we tell participants that our job is to create a stimulating environment, but that most of the content will come from them. At the graduation ceremony, they look back and realize that they learned more from their classmates than they did from the person at the front of the room. Creating that experience and crafting the environment takes a tremendous amount of discipline and thought.

Rhonda Spencer recalls a story about "feeding the hungry":

Group president Tim Sullivan came to me and said, "I need to get into that Leadership Fundamentals course. I need every leader in

my organization to get into that course." I was thrilled, because
Leadership Fundamentals was somewhat new then and some of our
organizational leaders were skeptical about the investment.

I said, "Wow, Tim, that's terrific. What is driving that thought?"

Tim said, "Mark Wachal." Mark was a leader in manufacturing
engineering at PCMC in Green Bay. He had a reputation for being
a tough but good leader. After Mark completed the first part of Leadership Fundamentals, he went back and quietly started to apply some
of what he had learned with his team. He realized that he needed to
change his communication and leadership style, rather than expecting others to conform to him.

After a few weeks, his team members said, "I don't know what
you are doing, but keep doing it." They had noticed the changes in
Mark. He was listening more, treating them with respect.

My response to Tim was, "Tim, we don't have a magic leadership
pill that we're giving people in Leadership Fundamentals. The course
is good, but it's not that good. The only explanation for the change
in Mark is that he was ready to change. We simply had the right tools
and the right environment to offer him at the right time to help him
change."

Tim attended his first Leadership Fundamentals graduation dinner to see Mark graduate. Mark got up and spoke with tears in his
eyes about how he had been changed by the experience. I looked over
at Tim, who also was impacted by the emotion of the event. In fact,
there wasn't a dry eye in the house.

The Selection Process

People have to apply to get into any of our in-person courses (though we do have some online courses that are available to everyone). We select those we believe have the highest potential because we know they want to be there, they are making a personal choice, and they will be great ambassadors of this content. We start with those we believe are strong enough to make a major personal change.

For Leadership Fundamentals, there is a long waiting list. The selection process includes several factors: What is your sphere of influence? Can you make immediate change? Do we think that you personally have the capacity to do that? Do we have the right mix of roles in the class? Do we have the right balance between office and manufacturing? Do we have the right mix between the front line and leadership? Do we have good gender balance? Do we have good divisional balance? All of these considerations factor into creating the cohorts.

We ask participants to set their organizational identity aside for the duration of the course; they don't know if the person next to them is a CFO or a plant leader. Coming in, participants get a workbook with everybody's photo and their responses to questions that they had received in advance. You get to see their thought pattern. At the beginning of the class, people introduce themselves; instead of biographical details, we ask them to share their thoughts about the most influential leader in their life, why they are here, and what they hope to get out of the experience.

We specifically say, "Please do not talk about your title or the actual day-to-day work that you do. We want to know who you are as a person." This sets them up for the journey of reflection they're going to go on throughout the class. Only over dinner or cocktails might they find out what somebody actually does. We emphasize that the class is about human connections—seeing people as people and not as their title.

It Begins with Communication

After we had been on our Lean journey for a couple of years, we started to reflect on what could drive that journey even deeper and more fully in our organization. One of the key statements in our continuous-improvement vision is that we should have regular sharing and listening through daily touch meetings; in those meetings people could talk about the work of the day, remove impediments, share improvement ideas, and deepen their connection with one another.

We brought a group of people together and asked, "What is the next thing we should look at?" We soon realized that we were struggling to communicate within the organization. It's not that we couldn't write e-mails or make PowerPoint presentations, but we were struggling to create strong relationships through good communication.

The Lean journey creates many more conversations than occurred before, requiring people to work together in cross-functional teams in whole new ways. We were taking people out of offices and putting them next to manufacturing associates. All this was creating a need in the culture for better ways to interact and communicate with one another. We researched outside courses, but none were suited to our needs. So we set out to create our own, and the result was our Communication Skills Training (CST) class.

A month later, Bart Hardy took CST at PCMC in Green Bay, Wisconsin. At the time, Bart was a front-line leader with about ten people on his team. When the class was announced, Steve Kemp, president of PCMC, knew it was something that would help Bart develop as a leader.

"Steve's always had a lot of confidence in me," Bart said. "But he's also pointed out that I wasn't always the best listener. I'm the guy who tries to do two, three things at the same time, but listening was never one of them."

The learning journey in CST is about understanding that though people think they're communicating, they've actually never been taught the mechanics of how to communicate or the effect that their communication has on others. It begins by diving deep into the communication cycle. What happens when the words leave my mouth and reach the person listening to the message? Then it goes deeper into why and how to actively listen, as well as how to think effectively about confrontation.

A few years later, Bart was promoted to vice president of Major Machinery where he now leads a team of 300 people. Bart came into the new role at a time when trust in the company's leadership was low. "There was a lot of tension," Bart said. "I walked into an environment where leaders and workers were not on the same page. In a work environment, there's often that natural tension, but this was much worse."

On the advice of one of the labor leaders, Bart scheduled one-on-one meetings with each of his 300 team members, spread out over seven months. Union reps were in the room to observe, but the conversations were between Bart and the team member. For his part, Bart asked two questions, "What are your expectations of leadership?" and "What prevents you from being more successful in your job than you currently are?" Then, using the techniques he learned in the CST class, Bart sat back and listened.

"I had some very brutal conversations," he said. "I tried not to be defensive about anything. I wanted them to be as open and honest as possible. Even if they could just vent, we'd see where it went."

In CST, the course mantra is "I am the message." We talk about how the vast majority of our communicating is nonverbal. Every part of who we are and how we move through the world—our gestures, our tone—creates the message that people receive, whether or not we intend to send it. You have to own the message that you send and think about how it impacts other people.

The team's response to a safe space in which they could express themselves to a fully engaged listener was amazing. They took full advantage of the opportunity to articulate their feelings. The open dialogue slowly began to establish a new trust. "I figured that after five or six people, I'd have a good idea of what the issues were and what I'd need to do," Bart said. "But what I saw was the impact it was having on *them*—that a leader would actually take the time to listen. It was just so refreshing. You could see what kind of difference it was making."

A year later, when it was time to negotiate a new contract, Barry-Wehmiller approached the union and asked if their contract could be extended by three months due to an issue that was occurring outside of PCMC. The union offered to extend it for three years; the only thing to negotiate was the wage scale for the term of the contract.

"It's hard to quantify trust," Bart said, "but that kind of blanket extension rarely happens with a labor agreement. "There were many things that helped rebuild the bridge of trust. I was just a small part, but it shows that listening goes a long way." Bart's use of reflective listening not only helped his team by giving them a voice to make a difference in their workplace, it also broadened his perspective as a leader. "It was good for them, they got to bend my ear," Bart said. "But at the end of the day I got to interact with so many people and had so much information to work with. It was fantastic."

Most people come into CST thinking they are great listeners. This actually means "I'm good at receiving information and parroting it back." But true, deep listening is not about formulating a response or helping someone solve a problem; it is about being present to the needs of the other person. We take people through a variety of exercises that help them see that they shouldn't have a destination in mind when they're listening to somebody who comes to them with a problem or shouldn't be thinking about what they're going to say next.

The course is a deeply personal experience, and it makes people realize the damage they have done to the relationships in their life. It calls people to examine how they are as leaders for their teams, as parents (which can be pretty troubling), as spouses, and as members in their community groups.

Marsha Burns, one of our professors in Barry-Wehmiller University, took CST in her first week with our company. It was a particularly harsh revelation for someone who felt she was a good communicator, having spent thirty years prior to coming to Barry-Wehmiller teaching people how to lead in business. "The first ten minutes of the class stressed that this was about me and my life, not about my performance," she said. "It forced me to look at myself and my behavior strictly in light of my values. I did not like what I saw. It changed my marriage; it changed my life."

CST helped Shayne Roberts, culture and people development director at BW Papersystems in Phillips, Wisconsin, make a very subtle, but significant change in communication with his daughter, Caitlin. At the time Shayne was taking CST, Caitlin was attending the University of Wisconsin in Madison. They had weekly phone calls that Shayne described as more like exercises in data-mining than conversation. "Just by my nature, and maybe it's typical of any parent, when I talked to her, I tended to try to meet my needs as a worried dad," Roberts said.

" 'How's school going?' 'Are you keeping up with your work?' 'Do you need any money?' "

But one day, inspired by his CST class, Shayne did something different. He called to talk to Caitlin, and when her phone went to voice mail, Shayne left this message: "I love you." A couple of minutes later, Caitlin called back and told Shayne that his message made her cry while she was walking down a street in Madison.

"That is something I'm going to remember forever," Shayne said. "It was like a lightbulb went on."

It wasn't just telling his daughter he loved her that made such an impact, Shayne said, as that expression is common in his family. But that day, it was a direct, sincere statement for *her*; he wasn't looking for anything in return. It wasn't about meeting Shayne's needs by receiving information, it was about meeting hers.

"Listening to others is hard work," Shayne said. "It just doesn't come naturally to me. I'm still not very good at it, but I used to be terrible. The journey has been amazing, though. I almost feel like we should call CST 'Awareness Training,' because it starts with self-awareness. I have to always be aware of whether or not I'm truly listening or I'll go right back to my old way of communicating, which was a one-way street that was just about me."

If those who take CST can make the changes they need to make, they experience a dramatic impact, which creates fertile ground for the rest of our leadership curriculum to take root. Over half the people in the company have taken this course; at some locations the figure is between 90 and 100 percent. Communication Skills Training has had a huge impact on our culture and has created a shared vocabulary for recognizing and avoiding communication pitfalls.

The way we actualize caring is through empathetic listening. That's why CST is the foundation of everything we teach at Barry-Wehmiller. If we really believe we can use the power of business to dramatically impact the world in a positive way, it has to start with a base understanding of the people around us. And that begins with listening.

Leadership Fundamentals

After launching CST, we turned our attention to developing a robust leadership curriculum around our leadership checklist. We worked with Chris Long, a former professor from Washington University in St. Louis, who is now a faculty member at Georgetown University, who helped us validate the content based on academic research. We developed and ran a "proof of concept" with four modules and asked leaders for feedback. Resoundingly, the group told us, "We love this, we want more of it. Please develop this class. We believe that we need to challenge people to practice, so let's teach it in three parts: a week in class with the group, six to eight weeks to practice what you've learned, and then come back together for the last section."

That was the birth of Leadership Fundamentals. So far, we have offered it about twenty times with a maximum of twenty-five people in each class. A very unique aspect of the class is in the deployment. One of our early decisions was to focus on front-line leaders. We know that 80 percent of our organization reports into that front-line layer, so from the very first class we said, "We want the very best team leaders in the organization; for them this would be a tremendous honor." Over the years, we've realized that demand for the class runs the gamut from individual contributors who are aspiring leaders to senior leaders in the organization, such as CFOs and others from the C-suite.

Matt Whiat is a decorated ex-Air Force officer who joined our

Organizational Empowerment group in 2013. He took our Leadership Fundamentals course and had the following reaction to it:

> *The military is charged to protect our Republic at all costs, even if that cost is life itself. The leadership training I received in the military reflected this overriding call to duty and manifested itself in the underlying motive of mission accomplishment. In other words, take care of your people so they can take care of the mission.*
>
> *The Barry-Wehmiller training diverges from that right at the beginning, with the very motivation that called for its creation. Barry-Wehmiller begins leadership training with the rallying cry that the way we treat our team members in business can have a dramatic and profoundly positive role in our society, that through leadership we can not only make a difference in our workplaces, but a dramatic difference in our society. And that this leadership training is not about increasing profits, decreasing waste, reducing overhead, or raising the productivity of workers. Throughout the training, there was not one single mention of any of these factors. No one, not the participants or the instructors, alluded to an increase in efficiency or a decrease in cost. Not one word was expended on how this is "good for business."*
>
> *I expected to see examples of factory situations in which employees were not meeting quotas or a case of a disgruntled saleswoman who is not meeting targets and her colleagues are forced to pick up the slack. Instead, most examples, both written and brought up by the attendees and the professors, were from outside of work. They were about the treatment of people in our everyday lives.*
>
> *Another monumental difference: In my Air Force training I was always segregated with my peer group. I learned with colleagues at a*

similar stage in their career. My more senior courses were driven by my acceptance into the higher ranks and positions of leadership. During Leadership Fundamentals, not only were the positions within the company of the attendees not known, they were never discussed! Only through informal discussions did I learn that some members were on the production floor building machines while another held the position of CFO within one of the business entities. Even the introductions purposely shied away from these labels, with each member answering questions such as "Who was the most influential leader in your life?" and "Besides your family, what do you value most in your life?"

After part one, I remarked how impressed I was with the instructors, the content, and the motivation for the course, which was centered on developing a society where people cared about each other first. There was not a hint of any ulterior motive. Having a few weeks between the two parts was a great time for application and reflection. Part two built on the momentum of the first part and never let up.

Creating the environment for the Guiding Principles of Leadership to be developed is one thing. Encouraging a "leadership checklist" (why doesn't every organization have one of these?) is another step along that cultural journey, but I was delighted to be a part of a class that was developed to explain in detail each one of the statements in these documents. Not just a line about being inspirational, but soul-searching discussions and exercises for hours on that concept. The power of the participants all being there of their own volition is incredible. It made for some of the most open discussions I've ever participated in. Not just goals and concerns, fears and aspirations, but participants willing to share deep, soulful admissions, leaving a broken trail of bravado and insecurities in their wake.

I've been in leadership positions for most of my adult life, and this course was so unconventional as to give me pause to reflect on the past and future. Like a great book or movie, this is a sign of something impactful—that long after you have left behind the pages, the theater, or the classroom, you are still pondering the teachings and the shared experience. But don't take my word for it. Ask the impressions of the CFO and three incredibly talented individuals who developed and ran multimillion-dollar organizations before joining the Barry-Wehmiller family. They were just as impressed and moved as the front-line leader and engineer sitting on my left and right. People don't shed tears and drop their lifelong armor on a whim.

Teaching the Whole Person

Peter Nicholson was an aftermarket sales leader who now leads our Accraply site in the United Kingdom. In the middle of the first week of Leadership Fundamentals, he said to the class, "You know, everyone at work calls me Peter, but at home I am Pete, and I am a completely different person. This is the first time it has ever occurred to me that I have permission to be Pete at work." The discussion centered on the energy it must take for him to maintain the façade of Peter at work when his true essence was to be Pete. It was a revelation and a great relief to him that he could be the same person in both places.

Matt Nichols, of our BW Papersystems organization in Phillips, Wisconsin, phrased it thus: "Do you know what it's like to feel like you have to put on a mask at work? For the first time in my career, I feel like I don't have to do that, that I can be my true self."

The way we create that experience for people is through the idea of disclosure. In Professor Training, our professors are trained to share their stories. We believe that real people telling real stories creates real learning. We do it in a couple of ways: first, simply by demonstrating that if you share your story, other people will want to do the same. We use a modified John Maxwell concept called the "Law of the Lid." Maxwell, an expert on leadership, talks about how leadership sets an upper limit. We talk about it in terms of the classroom. If you as a facilitator are at a 4 in terms of self-disclosure, your class will not surpass that; they will likely stay at or below a 3. If you disclose more about yourself and share your stars and your scars, the good things and the bad things that have happened to you as a leader, and you are at a 10 in disclosure, then you raise the lid on the classroom. We also teach storytelling: How do you take an experience in your life and craft a compelling story out of it?

A traditionally minded HR leader who was in Professor Training said to us, "You don't understand. Every shred of my HR training is telling me that you don't do this: You don't intentionally provoke this level of emotion in people; you don't disclose the failures of your past. If that were to happen in a meeting at my company, we would immediately pull that person out. If someone created a moment with that much emotion, we would shut it down right away. And now you're telling me that is my sole responsibility as a professor in front of this classroom."

Our response to that was, "Yes, that is exactly what we're telling you. As the embodiment of the leadership behaviors that we want to teach, you have to disclose your own personal journey. That often brings with it a great deal of emotion." Our courses are filled with emotional stories that make people tear up, as well as things that are frustrating or joyful.

Thriving Organizations Are Learning Organizations

Of all the things we have done to embed, strengthen, and perpetuate our unique culture, Barry-Wehmiller University may be the most significant. Through this journey, we have developed a growing appreciation for the power of continuously learning and growing our leadership capacities. The experiences people have shared in our courses have created deep connective tissue that binds our organization together with incredible strength. Through these courses, we learn from each other, and we learn to care more deeply for each other. We have earned the trust of our colleagues, who believe that what we have to teach is worth learning.

We strongly recommend that every company should develop its own version of BWU. We believe the fundamental differences in our approach have been integral to our success, to the impact we have been able to make on the organization and its people: having associates do all the teaching; using an opt-in model rather than requiring people to take certain courses; creating deeply immersive, interactive experiences; and making the courses relevant to people's whole lives, not just their work.

Chapter 13

| Everybody Truly Does Matter |

We opened the book with the story of one of our older acquisitions, PCMC. We close with the story of Baldwin, a company our "hybrid" equity arm Forsyth Capital (introduced in Chapter 3) acquired as one of its first investments in 2012, and some thoughts on the universal principles that can be gleaned from our journey. The story of that acquisition shows how our approach can be successfully applied by a new leadership team in a different industry globally.

—

Rich Bennett was the prototypical "manager" at the Baldwin plant in Lenexa, Kansas, a tough guy with an iron fist, the enforcer. He managed his plant with unquestioned power. Not a day went by that Rich didn't get nose to nose with employees, his spit drying on their cheeks and his threats ringing in their ears. Their offenses usually amounted to nothing more than taking five extra minutes at the water cooler and asking a coworker how their weekend was. It was a way of managing that Rich's supervisor had passed on to him and that Rich would eventually pass on to others.

If something difficult needed to be done, Rich was the man to do it—like the day he was asked to take ten people into a conference room and fire them. He was tough and driven and understood the game as it was played at a very typical, traditional US public company where, as he put it, "only the strong survive: You eat your young and do whatever you have to do to stay employed."

Rich joined Baldwin in 2002, got laid off in December 2004, and was rehired in 2007. He recalls, "We had no culture. Actually, it would be more accurate to say that we had a terrible culture. Our culture was that you had to succeed so that you wouldn't get fired, versus succeeding for the good of the business. You stepped on whoever you needed to step on, confronted whatever situation needed to be confronted. As much as you hated doing it and as much as it made you feel sick inside, it was what you had to do as a part of that leadership team. I was always exhausted and dreaded coming to work, because you never knew when the next crisis would hit."

Baldwin is a nearly hundred-year-old company with a proud heritage. It was founded in 1918 in Baldwin, New York, by ex-printer and press service technician William Gegenheimer in his garage. Gegenheimer invented a device he named the Baldwin Press Washer that reduced the time required to clean printing presses from hours to minutes. The invention became the key to the growth of offset printing. Baldwin grew to serve the high-volume, high-run printing market globally, focusing on newspapers and magazines.

After a public stock offering in 1987, Baldwin entered a period of steady growth in revenues and profits, earning a strong reputation for innovation, product quality, and customer support. The stock price climbed from $2.00 in 1987 to $14.25 in September 1989. Layoffs and rehiring came and went with business cycles. In 2009, in the wake of the Lehman collapse, revenues plummeted and 115 employees were let go. By end of 2011, revenues were further down, profits were a distant memory, and the share price had crashed to $0.48 a share.

The death spiral had begun. Morale was terrible. The culture had become deeply toxic. The company was cutting expenses, selling off assets, and consolidating facilities. Team members were being fired, but units were spending exorbitant amounts of money to air-freight equipment to meet short-term revenue targets. Business units operated as silos based on geography. Communication was poor and mostly negative. Information about what was really happening was hard to come by. It was like flying an airplane through a storm with no windows, no instruments, and no one on the radio. Nobody wanted to step up and lead. The atmosphere was full of fear and distrust.

Like many distressed public companies, Baldwin had become focused on the short term and driven by the quarterly expectations of the market. The company was out of compliance in its banking relationships; bankers were another set of people, in addition to Wall Street analysts, who were banging on them for better performance. The writing on the wall was clear: If a new owner didn't come in and rescue the business, it would soon be bankrupt, with little hope of recovery. Fortunately for the people of Baldwin, Forsyth bought the company in 2012.

—

Baldwin had endured years of traditional restructurings: selling real estate for cash, consolidating facilities, reducing headcount, and placing excessive demands on employees and suppliers. The leaders of Forsyth were confident they could help Baldwin shape a future of value creation. Through each previous restructuring, Baldwin associates had been told "it is going to be different this time." They were understandably cynical by the time Forsyth acquired the business.

The first message Forsyth conveyed was, "Trust us. We are in this for the long haul, and things are going to be OK. We care about you and we will be patient." The message was music to the ears of the weary people at Baldwin, but it seemed too good to be true.

Some leaders who had been with the business for a while said, "You guys are being too patient. People feel too safe now."

Kyle Chapman, Forsyth's managing director and now CEO of Baldwin, responded, "That doesn't make any sense. We're not saying you don't have to work. We're just saying you don't have to fear for your job. We want leaders to step up and lead and take risks and do things that can help push this business forward versus hiding in the corner so that they won't be next on the chopping block. The onus is on us to provide a better future for these folks. They did not create the position they are in. Past practices did. We are determined to provide them a new future."

Forsyth focused immediately on team building and creating a "one company" identity. They treated people the same way regardless of whether they happened to be German or Japanese or English. Closely hewing to the Barry-Wehmiller playbook, Forsyth looked for an opportunity to quickly demonstrate that things would be different. They didn't have to search very hard. Baldwin makes ultraviolet lamps as part of its core product line in the United Kingdom. The key to this kind of business is short lead times, ideally less than five days. Because of a production bottleneck, the lamp department had a forty-one-day lead time! So they were losing a lot of sales while by being pushed by management to grow sales to meet market expectations.

The leaders of the unit had repeatedly asked for approval to buy a $75,000 furnace that would eliminate a key bottleneck in the process. The request had been denied due to the intense focus on preserving cash and cutting costs. When Kyle Chapman saw the request, he approved it in about seven minutes—before Forsyth even formally owned the business. The new leaders didn't stop there; they organized a continuous-improvement event around the lamp-manufacturing process, lowering lead time to three days. Over the next year, revenues from the product line grew 20 percent.

Kyle recalls, "Doing that was simple. We listened to the people, empowered them, and trusted them. Of course, our lead time went down, and we benefited from growth and other operational improvements, but the amount of appreciation and morale boost we got from that simple action was huge. This was an organization pressured for earnings and cash but unable to implement even the most obvious initiatives that could begin to create value."

Remember Rich Bennett? He had a job offer from another company just prior to the acquisition. The new leaders recognized his potential and made a serious effort to keep him. He agreed to stay, but remained unconvinced that things would really change: "Once I learned who Bob Chapman was and what was going on, I did Internet research on him and watched all his speeches. My first impression was 'This guy is just out of his mind. You can't run a company like that. This guy is in la-la land. He doesn't know how the real world works.' In hindsight, staying is probably the best decision I ever made."

Rich was part of a group invited to visit several Barry-Wehmiller businesses, and his skepticism soon dissolved. "I jokingly called it the honeymoon tour. It happened just two weeks after the acquisition; somehow, they managed to get sixteen leaders from Japan, Germany, Sweden, Australia, and the UK all together. We got on the company jet and went from place to place. It was pretty overwhelming, but it gave us a lot of comfort that they know what they're doing and they've been there before. There was a lot of work to be done, but they assured us, 'Don't worry, guys, it's going to be fine. We've done this fifty times before; we know what we're doing. Just follow the game plan.' That was 100 percent accurate. They've done everything they said they were going to do."

To get Baldwin to operate as one company, Forsyth eliminated compensation models based on divisional performance. They focused on creating greater visibility of financials within the organization, not so they could fire underperformers, but to craft better strategy and use the metrics for coaching and to catch people doing things right. They restored a sense of pride by making it clear that the company would no longer chase revenue and do stupid things to get it. Salespeople were told, "We don't have to win every project. We need to enter into responsible relationships with responsible people who value what we bring to the table." As all Barry-Wehmiller businesses emphasize, Baldwin reconnected with its existing customers, increased service levels, and started paying closer attention to the decades of equipment that it had installed.

Within thirty months, Baldwin was well on its way to stability and steady growth. People throughout the organization had more hope and felt more connected to Baldwin than ever before. They are invigorated and almost in disbelief at the new markets Baldwin is opening up outside of printing. Before, they couldn't make trips to explore applications for Baldwin's technology. Today they are told, "Go open new doors, try new things. Don't worry about failing."

True to the Barry-Wehmiller approach, Forsyth didn't back up a truck full of leaders or helicopter in somebody from a different industry to come in and fix the business. They said they would do this with the folks from within, and they did. There are plenty of great leaders in every company we acquire; we just have to know how to find them and liberate them.

———

Rich Bennett sees his job now as giving everybody who was with Baldwin in the bad times the opportunity to do what they want to do in the rest of their professional lives. "If that means that you want my job, we'll figure out how to get you there. In my daily work and in potential acquisitions, that's what I look for: What kinds of opportunities does this bring to the people in our company and for their families? I feel like I can finally be my true self at work, part of a business that is about more than the bottom line."

Rich's home life has also changed. It's the classic story. "The stress level and the constant fear of losing your job—you try not to take it home, but of course you do. Now I feel like my life's made a 180-degree transition and I've won the lottery. My wife and I have taken longer vacations than ever before because I feel like I can be away from the business."

Kyle Chapman reflected on the experience and what it has meant to the people of the business and to him: "Our performance and the sustainability of our performance are healthier than they've ever been. We're hiring again. What I am fulfilled by is hearing people say how they feel about coming in to work. There is no other KPI [key performance indicator] that you can have that is greater than people saying they are happy and they are fulfilled. They love coming to work on Mondays. The sense of joy and enthusiasm is quite palpable. Money obviously matters, and profits are important. But it is not the only thing that matters. You have all these other sources of energy and inspiration and satisfaction. It is a ton of fun watching a historically great business be resurrected. It is very fulfilling to us. It's like restoring classic cars. We are restoring classic businesses and bringing them back to that sense of pride and relevance and having a future."

—

We make some of the best industrial machinery in the world. But I will not go to my grave being proud of all the machines we have built. Instead, I will be deeply grateful for all the lives that we touched and uplifted in our journey. The machinery we build is just the economic engine that enables us to touch lives. The flourishing of those lives is our paramount concern.

We wrote this book to share the wisdom we have been fortunate to acquire in a forty-year leadership journey, the essence of which can be boiled down to two simple words: *Everybody matters*. We want to help leaders in every field everywhere use this wisdom to be able to lead lives of meaning and fulfillment for themselves and to make the world a better place for those they impact through their leadership. We want to show everyone that business can be done in a better way, that when you pay people fairly and treat them superbly, you can not only compete globally but also enrich and elevate the lives of *everyone* the business touches.

Everybody truly does matter. No idea could be simpler or more powerful. It is an idea that has unlimited potential, because people have unlimited potential—to surprise, delight, and elevate themselves, each other, and all the world. Listen to the words of a young lady named Nikki Louder—child of a drug-addicted mother, made pregnant by her mother's boyfriend, a runaway living on the street, sleeping under bridges, scared, completely alone—who one day discovered an organization called Every Monday Matters, where she finally heard the words "you matter":

> *The words "you matter" changed everything about me. I'd never heard from anybody that I mattered. It was the [most] significant, altering moment of my life. Every child needs to hear that they matter. They need to hear it at breakfast, they need to hear it at lunch, they need to hear it at dinner. It's something that should be written on postcards and sent to everybody. You should have to say it twice a day. It's literally like just saying, "I love you;" it's that intention. And now if it's in every school and if it's with every child, now it gets passed to the home life and now it's with every brother and it's with every sister, and now it gets passed to their parents and now it's with every mom and with every dad, and now it gets passed to their workplace and now it's with their coworkers and their boss. It's just this virus of love that could be spread with two words.*[1]

Of course, saying the words "You matter" is very powerful—just as there is great value in telling someone that you love them. But it doesn't mean much unless you actually *show* that you love them. At Barry-Wehmiller, our vision statement calls all of us to measure our success by the way we touch the lives of others. Do we live that daily? And is it succeeding? Jenny Copanos, the assistant controller at our BW Container Systems division in Romeoville, Illinois, made me see how deeply rooted our vision is when she spoke about her years with the company.

Jenny joined the Barry-Wehmiller organization as a temporary employee when she was twenty-five and just beginning her career. She always knew she wanted to be an accountant but, beyond that, wasn't sure where she fit in. "Growing up, I never found my niche," she shared. "I wasn't good at sports, didn't join clubs. I was a good student but that was it. I didn't have a lot of confidence in myself."

Once she joined the Barry-Wehmiller organization that began to change. "My leaders identified strengths I didn't know I had," Jenny shared. "They offered me work and experiences that allowed me to grow in my role. They mentored me and helped bring out my gifts and talents. Through the years, my leader has often told me that I'm worth my weight in gold. That's very empowering to me."

Twelve years after joining, Jenny leads a six- member team and is a professor for Barry-Wehmiller University's Communication Skills Training. She says, "I have so much confidence in myself now. I finally understand who I was meant to be. To think that people I work with saw what I had been searching for my whole life is really amazing. I'm not sure I would have realized that anywhere else."

Jenny's marriage is richer as a result of her job. "I have been able to let down some of the barriers and open up to my husband, Nick, in ways that I couldn't early on in our marriage." It has also enhanced her relationship with her mother. "My mom and I get along even better now because I have become the person I want to be, not the person I thought she wanted me to be. Both she and my father are very proud of my accomplishments."

Jenny and Nick have almost three-year-old twins, Jackson and Addison. "I have learned how to be a better communicator, a better listener, and that will only help me as a parent," she reflected. "I don't come home from work stressed or angry; I truly feel a sense of fulfillment.

"I feel blessed to work for this company," she said, as her eyes welled with tears. "I am offered so much here. It makes me want to offer as much as I can to my team. My Barry-Wehmiller family was with me along my journey to discover my best self. I was always happy on the outside but there was something missing inside. Now I am happy on the inside too."

How do we know Truly Human Leadership is working? Just ask Jenny. Or Nick.

—

Our journey started with the realization that every day we have the opportunity to show people that we care. We do so by giving people the chance to be who they are intended to be—allowing them to discover, develop, share, and be appreciated for their gifts so that they go home knowing that *who they are* and *what they do* matter. In this way, our leadership actions daily affirm and demonstrate that everybody matters. When we show that we care, it becomes contagious; when people feel cared for, they naturally care for others.

By any measure, our company today is a thriving organization. Our people know that they work for a company that truly cares about them, a company with a secure future. They are inspired at work every day and return home to their families deeply fulfilled. This way of being is what will create the society we want for our children. I say to our people, "You don't just have a job. You have an opportunity to help create the world that you want your precious children to enter someday."

We realize that this is a journey. Our vision is aspirational, and we don't always live it perfectly. As in our continuous-improvement journey, it's about getting up every day and trying to be a little better than we were yesterday. It's about listening with humility, and working hard every day to close the gaps between our vision and everyday reality. With our manufacturing and engineering mind-set, we apply discipline to everything we believe in. Processes and systems remind us to do the things we intend to do as leaders every day; that's why checklists serve us so well. We don't wait for good things to happen by accident or *hope* that good work will be sustained. We work hard to ensure that our culture is alive and vibrant, as hard as we do in any other aspect of our business.

Steve Kemp is now the president of PCMC, the thoroughly demoralized and nearly bankrupt company that Barry-Wehmiller acquired in 2005, which we wrote about in the prologue. Ten years removed from the acquisition, Steve's appreciation for our approach has only grown: "At the end of the day, the message is that Bob Chapman cared about the people in Green Bay, Wisconsin. It wasn't about the numbers. He came in here with a very different mind-set, and believed in our people. He is constantly looking for companies that he can help realize their potential and create a stable future for their people. Most people who acquire companies are like buzzards who circle a company because they see an opportunity to make quick money. When they spot a company that is in trouble, they see weak prey and look to go in and devour it for themselves. Bob circles around struggling companies too, but he is like a guardian angel, thinking, 'How can we save this? How can we get this company back to what it once was? How can we release the potential that is still there, that they never came close to achieving, even in their heyday?'"

The mayor of Phillips, Wisconsin, embarrassed me once by pointing to me in a gathering and saying, "That man saved our town." I don't know if that is true, but I do believe it is true to say that our emphasis on human flourishing has had a multigenerational impact on the communities in which we operate. Most of our companies are a big part of a small community; if they cease to exist, it would devastate the community and could indeed mean the end of the town. So our way of doing business, in which everybody matters, has literally rescued many communities from the brink of disaster.

On one of his several visits to Barry-Wehmiller, Simon Sinek held up a mirror to us and said, "What you have is a blueprint. What you have evolved through trial and error is a vision that there could be something better. This now stands as an example of a different way to live. Not work. A different way to live. One other company, regardless of their size and regardless of their industry, will see it and say, 'That's interesting.' It won't be perfect and it won't be easy, but they'll give it a try, and then they'll tell another company. And they'll give it a try. This nation was founded on an idea. Don't forget that in other countries when you take an oath, you take an oath to protect the borders. In this country, you take an oath to protect the constitution. You take an oath to protect an idea. This company is a reflection of the founding of this country. It is a distinctly American company."

Our cultural journey began with the simple idea of making work more fun. From that modest beginning, we have shaped a culture that's now being watched and emulated nationally, even worldwide. We have come a very long way in just over a decade and a half. Imagine where we can be in another few decades. But more importantly, imagine the impact if these ideas take root and we are able to start a global epidemic of caring, inspiring, and celebrating.

It Is About Caring, Inspiring, Celebrating

A couple of years ago, I was asked to speak at an event organized by a $20 billion company. In the audience were leaders from all around the world. As I walked out, I saw two women standing next to the camera man, crying. I said hello to them and walked down the corridor with one of our sales executives.

I asked her, "Was my speech that bad?"

She said, "No. During your presentation one of them leaned over to me and asked, 'Do you work for Barry-Wehmiller?' I said, 'Yes I do.' She said, 'Is it really like that there?' I said, 'Yes it is.' She began crying and said, 'I wish I worked for a company like that.'"

Today the brokenness of the world is the news. We're inundated twenty-four hours a day with bad news because "what bleeds leads." Our culture at Barry-Wehmiller is so full of caring and recognition and celebration and holding up the goodness in people that the brokenness gets drowned out by the goodness. I know of no other company that focuses as much as we do on the goodness in people or that believes in it as much. There seems to be an inexhaustible supply of it; the more we shine a light into every corner of our organization, searching for goodness, the more we find it.

People often ask, "Bob, how can we do this? Where do we start?" It starts with caring about the people you lead, which means listening deeply to them and inspiring them to share their gifts fully. We then celebrate their journey toward our shared goals, in ways that are thoughtful, timely, and proportional. Those three words capture much of what we have learned on this journey: caring, inspiring, and celebrating.

Never look at the people you have been given the privilege to lead as functions—receptionists or engineers or accountants. See each one as a full human being, somebody's precious child, someone with infinite potential, whose life you have an opportunity to profoundly impact. We have a deep responsibility to be good stewards of that life. We want to send them home safe; we want them to be healthy, and we want them to be fulfilled—not just happy, but fulfilled, which means that "who I am" matters and "what I do" is valued and recognized.

That attitude of caring for people and sending them home fulfilled fosters a spirit of altruism; if I genuinely care about you, you will genuinely care about Mary, and if you genuinely care about Mary, she will genuinely care about Eli, and so on. The cycle of caring begins with you.

Caring has no hierarchy. Caring goes to the essence of who we are as human beings. Caring is universal; it works in unionized and non-unionized workplaces, in manufacturing and in service businesses, in high tech and low tech. It works beautifully in our 900-person consulting company, as it does in India, Germany, Italy, and France.

We truly do measure success by the way we touch the lives of people—not just our customers and employees, but everybody we touch. We inspire people to go out into our communities and get involved with organizations they feel contribute to making our communities more caring places.

A long-serving board member of Barry-Wehmiller recently remarked, "People have a sense of pride in working here. We're good and we are proud and we are big now. But we are big because we are good."

Beyond Self-Interest: An Ethical Foundation for Capitalism

Early capitalism was rooted in Judeo-Christian morality, as most business founders and leaders were religious individuals who brought those values into their work. Jerry Zandstra, an ordained minister and co-founder of The Inno-Versity Group, points out, "There is a very long tradition of the relationship between Judeo-Christian moral philosophy and the market economy. The earliest economists were monks from the school of Salamanca, thinking about how families could provide for themselves. In the sixteenth century, John Calvin was one of the first theologians to understand that capital has a cost and that charging interest, within reason, was not usury but actually necessary to a market economy. Adam Smith (the author of *Wealth of Nations*) was not an economist but a moral philosopher. His first book was called *The Theory of Moral Sentiments*. The industrial revolution did power things for production, but unfortunately it also changed how we thought about human beings. They became 'resources' or 'commodities.' We haven't changed much since."[2]

As we moved into a more secular world in the nineteenth and twentieth centuries, economists and other academics increasingly started to define the purpose of business purely in terms of profit. Capitalism lost its ethical foundation and became strictly amoral (not immoral), making no reference to "doing the right things for the right reasons." Whatever sense of morality remained was limited to staying within the law (which varies over time and by location). But morality and legality are not equivalent ideas. Any sphere of human activity that touches other humans (or indeed any other forms of life) must have a moral/ethical foundation; otherwise it inexorably drifts toward objectification and exploitation. That is precisely what has happened to business and capitalism.

Separating markets from morals was a deadly development. It caused enormous needless suffering for individuals and their families, and grievous harm to many communities, species, and the environment. It is imperative that we reconnect markets and morals. We must never sacrifice a higher value for a lower value, and the highest value of all is human flourishing. Our message is about morality ahead of money, people and purpose ahead of profits, the primacy of human flourishing over all else.

The ethical and moral standards humans adhere to can vary based on the environment they are in. The famous Milgram experiments about human obedience to authority figures showed that many people are quite willing to engage in behaviors that conflict with their own conscience when pressured to do so by those in charge.[3] Our inner demons are always waiting to surface in the right circumstances, but so too are "the better angels of our nature." We humans are capable of wanton, heedless acts of destruction. We are also capable of extraordinary, almost divine acts of caring and creation. Organizations and families alike can create conditions that foster the latter and suppress the former—or vice versa.

To promote human flourishing, organizations of all kinds and in every sphere of human activity must cease to think of themselves as entities designed to *use* people in pursuit of their own self-interested goals; they should see themselves instead as vehicles of service. They should attend to their own interests by serving their stakeholders rather than devising ever more sophisticated ways to manipulate, manage, and control those stakeholders.

We see broken lives and broken families all around us and wonder "What is happening to our youth?" Isn't it obvious? We don't value people enough, and we willfully shut our eyes to the impact we have on them. We use them and abuse them and degrade their sense of self-worth, leading to collateral damage on all the lives that they in turn touch. It is not a stretch to say that we are destroying our civilization by allowing organizations to be all about products, processes, and numbers. They need to be about people, purpose, and performance in thoughtful harmony and balance.

Business can be the primary vehicle for building a better world, if we appropriately respect and care for people. Business is far more than a profit machine. It is a vehicle for self-expression, for dreaming about and creating the future we desire, for accomplishing together what we cannot do alone, for creating extraordinary amounts of value of many kinds for everyone a business touches.

Business is a powerful instrument that we must use to serve the noble cause of greater human and planetary flourishing. Our greatest challenge is the widespread acceptance of a mercenary and apathetic approach to business. Legendary cartoonist Herb Block once said, "The worst form of corruption is the acceptance of corruption." People have become desensitized and resigned to the idea that "this is just how it is." There are huge financial incentives that keep the status quo locked in place. We have come to view unconscionable, selfish, and inhumane conduct as acceptable, normal, even laudable. This is not who we are. This is not what we want for ourselves and our children and grandchildren. We can and we must do better. What it will take is courageous, enlightened, truly human leadership.

Listen to the Wizard Within

When I share the story of our leadership journey with business leaders across the country, I rarely encounter any who think being good stewards of the lives in their organization is not the right way to lead. However, most think it is a difficult, even an impossible journey on which to embark.

Several years ago, I was speaking to a global gathering of executives of a major consumer products company. At the end of my presentation, a gentleman in the audience said, "Bob, I thoroughly agree with what you're saying. But how do you suggest we get our corporate leaders on board? How do we get them to let us begin?"

I replied, "Since when do you need a memo from corporate that tells you that it is acceptable to be good stewards of the lives in your care?"

It reminds me of a lesson from *The Wizard of Oz*. Dorothy, Toto, the Scarecrow, the Tin Man, and the Lion follow the yellow brick road in search of the great Wizard who will surely provide what each is missing: a way back to Kansas, a brain, a heart, and courage. They reach the castle of the mystical, magical Wizard and hear his thunderous voice booming from behind the curtain. They are frightened but excited at the prospect of figuring out how to finally attain what they've been seeking. Suddenly Toto jumps from Dorothy's basket and pulls back the curtain, revealing the great Wizard behind. And, lo and behold, he's just an ordinary man. Although not a magical wizard, this ordinary man proves to be very wise. He helps Dorothy and her companions see that what they were looking for was actually within them all along.

Embark on your journey now. You don't need a memo from the almighty wizards of corporate to tell you that it's OK to do the right thing. A spreadsheet can't show you how to treat people. No executive order is required to allow you to pause each day to have a thoughtful conversation with someone in your organization. Listen to them. Show them that what they do and who they are matters. You—and everyone else in your organization—already have everything within yourselves to start living the universal truth that everybody matters.

Epilogue: It's All About the People

While our path to discovering the power of truly human leadership has been unique, filled with moments of awakening to fresh and powerful insights, we can point to certain universal principles that can guide any team that embarks on this journey. These principles will continue to guide us in the future:

Every human being matters, and is unique. We human beings are endowed with astonishing, almost divine capacities, and each of us holds the potential for greatness. Viktor Frankl taught us that the ultimate question is not what we expect of life; it is what life expects of us, which is the full realization of our potential. As individuals and as leaders, we have a responsibility to live our lives and lead others in such a way that our extraordinary capacities for action, caring, and creativity are able to find joyous expression. We have paid people for their hands, and they would have given us their heads and hearts for free if we had only known how to ask. As Herb Kelleher, the beloved longtime CEO of Southwest Airlines, said, "The business of business is people. Yesterday, today, and forever."

Evolution has a purpose. Things unfold the way they do for a reason. Rabbi and integral wisdom philosopher Marc Gafni writes, "The universe is moving toward ever-higher levels of love, recognition, mutuality, and embrace." Martin Luther King Jr. recognized that "The arc of the moral universe is long, but it bends toward justice." We are each instruments of an evolutionary journey toward greater manifestations of the good, the true, and the beautiful. At every stage of this collective human journey, we are called on to play our role; we just need to have our minds and hearts open so we can rise to the occasion. Peter Koestenbaum puts it beautifully: "It is the future that pulls rather than the past that pushes." The entire human journey on this planet can be seen as one of gradually waking up to our own potential and divine nature. It has been a journey of rising consciousness: an ever-wider circle of care, a greater awareness of our interconnectedness and interdependence, a more finely developed sense of right and wrong, greater willingness to take responsibility for our actions, rejection of violence of all kinds, celebrating our diversity, and living in harmony with nature. We are becoming better aligned with what Lincoln called the "better angels of our nature." Individuals and organizations who are resonant with this evolutionary journey will thrive and enable the thriving of others, while those who are in disharmony with the journey will wither and perish.

The most powerful energy in the universe and thus in human beings and in organizations is caring. It starts with the profound recognition of the impact our words and actions have on the lives we have the privilege to touch. Every organization should be an instrument of service to humanity, a vehicle for human beings to experience and practice true caring. We grow and evolve and fulfill our unique purpose and destiny by finding richer ways to acknowledge our oneness and manifest our caring natures. There is no limit to this.

The more we can combine work and caring, the more fulfilled we will be and the further we will collectively advance. Freud said love and work are the cornerstones of our humanness. Adam Smith wrote of the two primary human drives: self-interest and the need to care. Viktor Frankl wrote of the sources from which true happiness ensues: doing work that matters, loving without condition, and growing from adversity. We must end the artificial separation between these two essential aspects of our beings and show up as a whole person in all that we do.

Individuals can choose to operate at a higher plane of consciousness or not. Growth in consciousness is not automatic. As Peter Koestenbaum puts it, "We have reached such explosive levels of freedom that we are in charge of our own mutation." When we make the choice to evolve, we can shape organizations to manifest greater caring. In turn, such organizations foster greater caring in the individuals who are touched by them. As Winston Churchill said, "First we shape our buildings and then our buildings shape us."

Organizations can be built for resilience and inspired to care. We can design and lead organizations so that they are aligned with the forces of positive change and reject attempts by retrograde leaders to move them away from caring. With sustained caring leadership and clearly articulated and deeply engrained values, organizations can develop an "immunity to negative change," a dynamic in which only forward movement is possible.

This is a journey with no end point. No organism or organization can remain healthy if it exists in stasis. Humans and organizations alike must continue to grow and evolve or they will perish. Regardless of how refined our understanding of truly human leadership becomes, we must continue to deepen and enrich it.

While these principles are universal, every individual and organization must develop unique expressions of these and continue to evolve over time.

Acknowledgments

Bob's acknowledgments

My deepest gratitude to the team members of Barry-Wehmiller, past and present, whose words, thoughts, and actions were the inspiration for our cultural rebirth and consequently this book. I appreciate your candor, your dedication, and your willingness to allow us to tell your stories. Thank you for helping me to see that the way I lead profoundly impacts the way you live.

My journey would not have been possible without my father, William Chapman, who placed his trust in me when he asked me to join Barry-Wehmiller in a leadership role. He was one of the first people to teach me a valuable lesson: Earning trust begins by extending trust.

I owe more than I can convey to Simon Sinek, friend, mentor, partner, for his constant affirmation of our message and his steadfast determination to help us change the world.

Special thanks to Srikumar Rao, who was one of the first to point out our responsibility to share our message of Truly Human Leadership with the world. Other special supporters who affirmed our message and encouraged us to share it were Bill Ury, Amy Cuddy, Dr. Charles Denham, Taavo Godtfredsen, Jim Selman, Eric Motley, Jerry Zandstra, and Lynne Twist.

Through the contributions of these special people—and many unnamed others along the way—my hope is that someday Truly Human Leadership will be the rule and not the exception and that our children, our grandchildren, and all future generations of precious children will have the opportunity to share their gifts in a place where they feel valued, inspired, and appreciated.

—RHC

Raj's acknowledgments

I have had the opportunity to study and learn from many wonderful companies through my work in the global Conscious Capitalism movement. I have found Barry-Wehmiller to be unique in the depth of its commitment to people and the context within which it is able to offer those people security, meaning, and fulfillment. It is a beacon of hope and optimism at a time of considerable despair.

Every book is a journey of discovery and growth. In the process of working on this book, we sought to tell the Barry-Wehmiller story and extract universal lessons from it that could help guide leaders in all spheres to create more fully human workplaces. For me, the book expanded and enriched my understanding of two of the four pillars of Conscious Capitalism: First, the idea that a company's higher purpose need not be restricted to its product; every company can and should strive to make the well-being of all the people it touches integral to its purpose. The second is that the impact of leadership extends beyond the workday and the work environment; the way people experience work has a direct impact on the well-being of their families and communities. The beautiful phrase that encapsulates the Barry-Wehmiller approach to leadership and business—"We measure success by the way we touch the lives of people"— is one that every organization in the world would do well to live by.

I was inspired by numerous individuals at many Barry-Wehmiller facilities in several countries. I would particularly like to thank the people I interviewed for this book, who generously shared their experiences and wisdom with us. In particular, I would like to thank Kyle Chapman, Rich Bennett, Sergio Casella, Ken Coppens, Jay Deitz, Randall Fleming, David Ives, Steve Kemp, Bob Lanigan, Bill Morgan, Carol O'Neill, Tim Sullivan, and Joe Wilhelm.

I would also like to thank Mary Rudder, Trevor Macdougall, and Matthew Whiat for their extraordinary commitment and many contributions to this project. I am grateful to my talented daughters Priya and Maya, who transcribed most of the interviews and helped with editing, and I thank my wife, Shailini, for her thorough proofreading of the manuscript and for her patience and understanding through this and other book projects. I would also like to thank Mr. Puran Dang for his encouragement and thoughtful comments on the manuscript.

Finally, I would like to acknowledge our great good fortune in working with a brilliant team at Penguin Portfolio, including Adrian Zackheim, our publisher, and Eric Nelson, our editor. Adrian was an early believer in the Barry-Wehmiller story and a tireless advocate for getting the message right. Eric joined this project when it was already under way and played a huge role in shaping the book. Thank you both for sharing your talents with us and caring deeply about this project.

—RSS

All Barry-Wehmiller proceeds from *Everybody Matters* will be donated to Our Community LISTENS, a nonprofit dedicated to bringing powerful Communication Skills Training to communities throughout the United States. To learn more, visit OurCommunityLISTENS.org.

For more information or assistance in building a people-centric culture, visit BWLeadershipInstitute.com.

Notes

Chapter 3: Growing the Human Side

1. From a talk by Simon Sinek at Barry-Wehmiller. Simon writes about the "circle of safety" in his book *Leaders Eat Last* (New York: Portfolio/Penguin, 2014).

Chapter 4: Leadership Is Stewardship

1. *Maritz Research Hospitality Group 2011 Employee Engagement Poll*, Research White Paper, June 2011, http://www.maritz.com/~/media/Files/MaritzDotCom/White%20Papers/ExcecutiveSummary_Research.pdf.

2. Anahad O'Connor, "The Claim: Heart Attacks Are More Common on Mondays," *New York Times*, March 14, 2006, http://www.nytimes.com/2006/03/14/health/14real.html.

3. Chronic Diseases and Health Promotion, http://www.cdc.gov/chronicdisease/overview/index.htm.

4. Towers Watson, "Engagement at Risk: Driving Strong Performance in a Volatile Global Environment," 2012 Global Workforce Study, July 2012, http://www.towerswatson.com/Insights/IC-Types/Survey-Research-Results/2012/07/2012-Towers-Watson-Global-Workforce-Study.

5. Samantha Cole, "The Terrible Things Your Work Stress Is Doing to Your Health: New Research Reveals How Work-Related Stress Translates to Life-Threatening Conditions—and How Employers' Attitudes Can Make It Worse," *Fast Company*, March 4, 2015, based on "The Relationship Between Workplace Stressors and Mortality and Health Costs in the United States," by Joel Goh, Jeffrey Pfeffer, and Stefanos A. Zenios, http://www.fastcompany.com/3043112/the-future-of-work/the-terrible-things-your-work-stress-is-doing-to-your-health.

6. *State of the American Workplace: Employee Engagement Insights for U.S. Business Leaders* (Gallup, Inc., 2013), http://employeeengagement.com/wp-content/uploads/2013/06/Gallup-2013-State-of-the-American-Workplace-Report.pdf.

7. Kamal Sarma remarks at Conscious Capitalism Australia conference, Sydney, June 24, 2014.

8. Sigal Barsade and Olivia O'Neill, "Employees Who Feel Love Perform Better," HBR Blog Network, January 13, 2014, https://hbr.org/2014/01/employees-who-feel-love-perform-better/.

Chapter 5: Hardwiring Our Culture

1. Tony Schwartz, "Why Fear Kills Productivity," *New York Times*, December 5, 2014.

2. Sigal G. Barsade, "The Ripple Effect: Emotional Contagion and Its Influence on Group Behavior," *Administrative Science Quarterly* 47, no. 4 (2002): 644–75; quote from p. 669.

3. C. Goodman and R. Shippy, "Is It Contagious? Affect Similarity Among Spouses," *Aging & Mental Health* 6, no. 3 (2002): 266–74; Jennifer Katz et al., "Individual and Crossover Effects of Stress on Adjustment in Medical Student Marriages," *Journal of Marital and Family Therapy* 26, no. 3 (2000): 341–51.

4. R. William Doherty et al., "Emotional Contagion: Gender and Occupational Differences," *Psychology of Women Quarterly* 19, no. 3 (1995): 355–71.

5. Shirley Wang, "Contagious Behavior," *Observer* 19, no. 2 (February 2006), http://www.psychologicalscience.org/index.php/publications/observer/2006/february-06/contagious-behavior.html.

6. Barsade, "The Ripple Effect."

7. Ibid.

8. Ibid.

Chapter 6: The Test of Our Culture

1. Samantha Cole, "The Terrible Things Your Work Stress Is Doing to Your Health: New Research Reveals How Work-Related Stress Translates to Life-Threatening Conditions—and How Employers' Attitudes Can Make It Worse," *Fast Company*, March 4, 2015, based on "The Relationship Between Workplace Stressors and Mortality and Health Costs in the United States," by Joel Goh, Jeffrey Pfeffer, and Stefanos A. Zenios, http://www.fastcompany.com/3043112/

the-future-of-work/the-terrible-things-your-work-stress-is-doing-to-your
-health.

2. "Financial Crisis of 2007–08," http://en.wikipedia.org/wiki/Financial_
    crisis_of_2007%E2%80%9308#Effects_on_the_global_economy.

3. Douglas A. McIntyre, "The Layoff Kings: The Companies That Cut the Most
    in 2008," 24/7 Wall St., December 20, 2008, http://247wallst.com/
    jobs/2008/12/20/the-lay-off-kin/.

4. Dan Oppenheimer, "George Packer: Don't CEOs Have Any Shame?" May 26,
    2013, http://www.salon.com/2013/05/26/george_packer_dont_ceos_have_
    any_shame/.

Chapter 7: Envisioning the Ideal Future

1. George Land and Beth Jarman, "Future Pull: The Power of Vision and
    Purpose," *The Futurist*, July/August 1992, 25.

2. Interview in Kim Ann Curtin, *Transforming Wall Street: A Conscious Path for a
    New Future* (Lake Placid, N.Y.: Aviva Publishing, 2015).

3. We calculate value creation using the well-accepted "Economic Value Added"
    share price methodology developed by Stern Stewart. This allows our team to
    "monetize" their vision to ensure they are creating economic value, which we
    recognize as critically important to our stewardship of the lives of our stake-
    holders.

Chapter 8: A New Way to Lead

1. John T. James, "A New, Evidence-Based Estimate of Patient Harms Associated
    with Hospital Care," *Journal of Patient Safety* 9, no. 3 (September 2013):
    122–28.

2. Atul Gawande, "The Checklist," *The New Yorker,* December 10, 2007, http://
    www.newyorker.com/magazine/2007/12/10/the-checklist.

3. BG Allen, "Be-Know-Do: The Army's Leadership Model," blog post, March 7,
    2011, http://bgallen.com/2011/03/07/be-know-do-%E2%80%93-the-
    army%E2%80%99s-leadership-model/.

4. Kevin Cashman, *Leadership from the Inside Out: Becoming a Leader for Life*, 2nd
    ed. (San Francisco: Berrett-Koehler, 2008).

Chapter 9: Humanizing the Process

1. Quoted in Sven Beckert, *Empire of Cotton: A Global History* (New York: Alfred A. Knopf, 2014).

2. Several reports cite Lean's extremely low success rate. For example, see "If Less Than 1% of Companies Are Successful with Lean," Business901 blog post, http://business901.com/blog1/if-less-than-1-of-companies-are-successful-with -lean-why-are-we-doing-it/; and "What Are the Barriers to Lean Success: Most Companies Are Using Lean, but Not Always So Well," *Supply Chain Digest*, January 30, 2013, http://www.scdigest.com/ontarget/13-01-30-2.php? cid=6680.

3. "What Is Lean?" Lean Enterprise Institute, http://www.Lean.org/WhatsLean/.

4. "5S (methodology)," Wikipedia, http://en.wikipedia.org/wiki/5S_(methodol ogy).

Chapter 10: Cultivating Responsible Freedom

1. Polly Labarre, "Do You Have the Will to Lead? Philosopher Peter Koesten-baum Poses the Truly Big Questions: How Do We Act When Risks Seem Overwhelming? What Does It Mean to Be a Successful Human Being?" *Fast Company,* March 2000, http://www.fastcompany.com/38853/do-you-have-will-lead.

2. "The Freedom Report: An Empirical Analysis of How Freedom Impacts Business Performance," LRN, 2014, http://pages.lrn.com/the-freedom-report.

3. Daniel Pink, *Drive: The Surprising Truth About What Motivates Us* (New York: Riverhead Books, 2009).

4. David Marquet, *Turn This Ship Around: A True Story of Turning Followers into Leaders* (New York: Portfolio/Penguin, 2013).

Chapter 11: Recognition and Celebration

1. Polly Labarre, "Marcus Buckingham Thinks Your Boss Has an Attitude Problem," *Fast Company*, August 2001, http://www.fastcompany.com/43419/ marcus-buckingham-thinks-your-boss-has-attitude-problem.

2. "Research Tips: Rewards, Recognition, Motivation and Turnover," Business Research Lab, 2013, http://www.busreslab.com/index.php/articles-and-stories/

research-tips/employee-satisfaction/rewards-recognition-motivation-and-turnover/.

Chapter 13: Everybody Truly Does Matter

1. "Nikki's Story," Every Monday Matters, https://www.youtube.com/watch?v=n-qsLcQNCXgk&feature=youtu.be.

2. Jerry Zandstra, private communication.

3. Stanley Milgram, "Behavioral Study of Obedience," *Journal of Abnormal and Social Psychology* 67, no. 4 (1963): 371–78. As long as a "higher up" said it was OK, people were willing to administer stronger and stronger electric shocks to real human subjects. Amazingly, 50 percent of them were willing to shock subjects to death, as long as the directive to do so came from a legitimate source and absolved them of personal responsibility.

Index